To Henk

(signature)

THE INDEPENDENT FACTOR

THE
INDEPENDENT
FACTOR

My Personal Journey
through Politics
and Diplomacy

Denis Worrall

ISBN 978-0-620-81629-8

Published by Author using Reach Publishers' services,
P O Box 1384, Wandsbeck, South Africa, 3631

Reach
PUBLISHERS

Blue Weaver Marketing and Distribution
021 701 4477
info@blueweaver.co.za

Also available on Amazon as a Kindle eBook and Paperback

*This book is dedicated to my beloved wife
Anita, our three sons, Christian, Lyndon and
Dean, and our grandchildren, Manon, Ella,
Kyla, Ty, Bear and Bibi*

"Denis has a story to tell – including the establishment of the Democratic Party, his international experience with leaders like Margaret Thatcher and Geoffrey Howe and, back home, Colin Eglin, F.W. de Klerk, Nelson Mandela and others. I found it gripping. A highly recommended read."

> – Bennie Rabinowitz, a leading Cape Town businessman, community leader and old friend

In an editorial under the heading "Arrival and Departure", the London *Times* wrote: "A persuasive advocate, brilliant debater, acknowledged student of international affairs, Ambassador Worrall was ideally suited to sell the government reform programme to British and international opinion." And the South African correspondent Stanley Uys wrote in his *London Dateline*: "Make no mistake about it, Dr Worrall has many well-wishers. Even his opponents concede that, in style and content, his ambassadorial performance was in a class of its own."

> – *The Times of London*

"Prime Minister Thatcher took over the direction of policy on South Africa with some help from me, and Ambassador Denis Worrall who was an invaluable source of information of debates within the South African government. Brilliantly written, *The Independent Factor* gives a penetrating view of UK–South African relations at the height of sanctions and the anti-apartheid movement."

> – Lord Charles Powell, former foreign affairs private secretary to Margaret Thatcher

"Denis Worrall's overwhelming interest in politics kindled his ambition to bring about change in South Africa, at a time when most of us were in despair. In this book, he provides many insights into his encounters, frustrations and triumphs after he made the decision to become actively involved in politics."

> – Professor Andrew Duminy

At a critical point in UK and EU relations with South Africa in 1986, Sir Geoffrey Howe was mandated to visit Southern Africa in the hopes of improving the situation. Sir Geoffrey reported that "Pretoria was reluctant to receive me. It was only after a strenuous private meeting with their excellent and liberal London Ambassador, Denis Worrall, that President Botha agreed to receive me. Ambassador Worrall's resignation from London drew wide media reporting in the UK and in South Africa."

> – Sir Geoffrey Howe, British Foreign Secretary
> in the Thatcher government

"I have read the whole book and congratulate you on a magnificent effort. You have had a truly wonderful life and have captured it very well. I found the section on your years in London riveting. As an Oxford man I must confess you got more out of the USA than I got out of Oxford! Well done, my boy."

> – Bill Yeowart, an old friend, biblio-
> phile and drinking companion

The decision to contest the Helderberg constituency received massive publicity. Typical was prominent independent columnist Max du Preez's comment under the heading "Worrall, Victory or Wilderness". "Dr Denis Worrall left his plum job to fight Cape National party leader Chris Heunis in a seat where the NP majority in 1981 was nearly 3,000. There are many other seats with better chances than that … A bad performance by Dr Worrall could take him into the political wilderness."

> – Max du Preez, South African author,
> columnist and documentary filmmaker

Gary Player demonstrated his support for Denis in Helderberg by attending a couple of meetings and playing a demonstration round in Somerset West. Denis played with him. Jannie Momberg writes: "I was truly thankful that the voters did not see their candidate play golf, as it would have spelt disaster!"

> – Jannie Momberg, founding member of the Democratic
> Party, former ANC member of Parliament, South
> African Ambassador to Greece

In his acceptance speech as leader of the Democratic Alliance, Tony Leon said, "We may be a small party, but we can be the pivot of a realignment – at the radical centre of our politics. And if you doubt that we can do it, remember what Denis Worrall once achieved from a far smaller base than ours is today."

– Tony Leon, South African politician,
leader of the Democratic Alliance

Dene Smuts writes in her book *Patriots and Parasites* of her interview with Worrall: "The interview left me convinced that he was sincere and acting out of a sense of duty, which is what I titled the resulting feature." It was this interview, whose publication was suppressed by Ton Vosloo of Naspers.

– Dene Smuts, editor of *Fair Lady*, interviewing Denis
Worrall in the middle of the Helderberg campaign

TABLE OF CONTENTS

FOREWORD BY DAVID GANT

The Rubicon speech of President P.W. Botha in August 1985 and the government's subsequent handling of the Coventry Four, the Eminent Persons Group and the KwaZulu-Natal Indaba deepened South Africa's already existing political, social and economic crisis. A continuation of the status quo could only lead to, and indeed did lead to, increasing unrest, economic regression, international isolation, deteriorating black–white relationships and even possibly civil war.

In the face of a government unwilling to initiate real reform, somebody, somewhere, somehow had to break the mould and provide a powerful and fresh message of political change in our country. And that is exactly what Denis Worrall did when he bravely swapped the comfort of diplomacy in London and the Court of St James for the uncertainties and risks of standing as an Independent candidate in the dramatic Helderberg election of 1987, the results of which resonated throughout our nation and paved the way towards a new political dispensation in our country.

And so this book is about those events and the life and times of this extraordinary South African diplomat and politician. But more importantly, it is a story about an individual whose career was shaped by family, friends, educators and others who, together with his exposure to a wide range of political acquaintances, some friendly, some adversarial, led him to exercise his personal conscience and political conviction and, with courage, make a massive contribution to the process of democratisation in South Africa. Internationally described as the 'Worrall factor', Denis spearheaded an initiative which proved that South Africans were ready to embrace political change and which provided essential momentum towards the non-racial, all-inclusive democracy that South Africa enjoys today.

Denis's contribution to that process was immense and his life story of academia, diplomacy and politics is to be highly welcomed and appreciated.

Dave Gant

Former founder and co-chairman of the Independent Party,
chairman of the Federal Council of the Democratic Party, and
former member of the President's Council
September 2018

FOREWORD BY IAN FARLAM

I am glad that my friend Denis Worrall has written the story of his life – and what an interesting life it is!

We became friends in my first year at UCT, where he was a popular student leader and the vice-chairman of the SRC. I first came across him in the debating society (of which he was the chairman) where his impressive debating skills marked him out as someone who would be able to make an important contribution to our national life by the eloquent and persuasive presentation of enlightened views on the issues of the day. That he did so comes out clearly in this book.

The major part of the book deals with his activities as a politician and diplomat and the important part he played in guiding (mainly white) public opinion towards the acceptance of meaningful change in our country. But the earlier part, dealing with his role as an academic, a political commentator, the founder and editor of an important and influential journal of public opinion, and the wide range of friends and acquaintances he had in South Africa and abroad with whom he shared views and insights on a variety of topics, provides the necessary background and explanation for the extraordinary role he played on what may be described as the left wing of the National Party and as the diplomat who influenced Margaret Thatcher in the stance she adopted towards South Africa.

Our paths crossed again when, after he entered Parliament, he resumed the legal studies he had put aside to concentrate on philosophy and political science, and commenced practice as an advocate at the Cape Bar.

The many strands which combined to constitute his intellectual formation, philosophy, political science and law, coupled with his debating skills, which were evident from the start, equipped him to achieve what he did in helping us to obtain the democratic constitutional state which had seemed impossible to achieve a short while before.

This is a book which deserves to be read by all who are interested in understanding an important part of our recent history.

I.G. Farlam
25 September 2018

PREFACE

When I resigned as Ambassador to the UK and returned to South Africa, I was overwhelmed with publisher's offers, which I declined on the basis that I expected to have a political life after London, as was indeed the case. Helderberg and the establishment of the Independent Party followed, as did the merger with what was then a declining Progressive Federal Party to form the Democratic Party under the leadership of Zach de Beer, Wynand Malan and myself. I stood down from active politics when Tony Leon, who I believe went on to play a major role in our democracy, became leader, as did Helen Zille after him. In the role that I chose for myself, as a consultant to international investors and foreign business companies, I obviously had to keep my ear and nose to the ground politically. But at that point I stepped out of active politics, which is why that part of my life is not part of this story.

I am now at an age when most people are retired. However, I describe myself, with my side-line business interests, and my beloved wife Anita still working a regular eight-hour day, as semi-retired. And so it was that I turned my attention to writing about my past, initially not too seriously. If asked what I was doing in my home study all day, I said I was writing something for my children and grandchildren.

Quite frankly, that is how this book began. I should add that I had some excellent props. Some individuals who read the manuscript have remarked on my ability to date and detail events and developments. There is a room in our house – it was meant to be a second spare bedroom – which is full of documents, speeches, files of news clippings, and over sixty annual diaries dutifully put together down the years by several super-competent personal assistants. Among them are Sharon Nixon, Felistia de Jäger, Sheila Harvey, Stacey Farao, Kamreya Clark and Deborah Bennett, who more recently organised them for easy access to the writer in residence. And I am most grateful to Deborah for having overseen every page of this book and prepared the index.

An Independent Factor is intended as a memoir, which, according to my dictionary, is a history or narrative composed from personal experience and memory. But what will be very evident from even a cursory reading of this book is that many people have contributed in important ways to it. Aside from being mentioned in the text, there are several who actually gave meaning to certain of my experiences. Dave Gant, who has shared so much of my political life, made a truly giant contribution to the writing of the book, as did Professor Andrew Duminy and Chris Reader. I thank Judge Ian Farlam for his greatly appreciated foreword. He clearly knows me much better than I thought. Persons who threw light on certain facets of my experience as I wrote include Barbara Bester, Bennie Rabinowitz, Keith Gurney, Charles Moore, Malvern van Wyk Smith, Gunter Steffens, Andre Botha, David Potter and Lord Charles Powell. I am grateful to Tim Hughes, whose excellent UCT master's degree dissertation on the 1987 general election was a very valuable resource. And I am sorry that I could not include some of the imaginative suggestions Max du Preez has made. I also owe thanks to Advocate Jan Heunis for his published views on the Coventry Four and to my former Embassy colleague André Pelser, who bore the brunt of that crisis. And finally I want to pay a very sincere tribute to the late Jannie Momberg, who really was the person to decide it would be Helderberg, and it is my deep wish that his feisty wife Trienie enjoy this book.

Writing has come easy to me all my life – whether it be chapters in political science books, newspaper columns or articles. Writing something like this is a very different story. I can confirm that. And absolutely essential therefore has been Russell Martin, my editor. I have accepted his advice on every point because I think he is extremely sensitive to a writer's needs and best interests.

Denis Worrall

1

THE BEGINNING

E very person has a story to tell. I have had a very varied career: executive trainee for an oil company; a judge's registrar; an advocate; an academic; a member of Parliament; editor and publisher of an intellectual review; a newspaper columnist; an ambassador; a director of companies; consultant to the World Bank; and, last but not least, a husband, father and grandfather. But my story is essentially a political one because I have always had a passion for politics, starting at an early age and probably influenced by my father, who had strong Cape views.

I studied politics both formally and informally. I researched politics; wrote about politics; and, for a time, practised politics. Politics involves choices and commitments, with concomitant loyalties and emotions, which in turn are influenced by an individual's social and economic background, religion and education, and so on. This is why most biographies or memoirs of people in politics detail their family backgrounds and histories. For instance, the fact that Margaret Thatcher was the daughter of a grocer and that the family lived above their shop in a small town called Grantham; or that Nelson Mandela was born into a royal family; that Lyndon Johnson was the eldest of five children in a dirt poor family; and that John F. Kennedy, by contrast, was born with a golden spoon in his mouth and had the best of political connections. These are all facts that political analysts have savoured and found relevant in some way or another to those leaders' attitudes and policies.

Without making comparisons, I judge that in order for readers to understand my life story, I would want them to know something more about me than that I am a white, middle-class South African male who has lived most of his life in a racially segregated and culturally and linguistically diverse society.

My life story begins in 1935, when I was born in a small town, now a city, called Benoni ('Son of Sorrow'), to the east of Johannesburg on the great gold-mining Reef, which formed the basis and origin of South Africa's industrial economy. My mother was Hazel (née Holdcroft), a local girl, the daughter of one of that remarkable group of Irish drapers – among them familiar South African family names like Garlick, Stuttaford, Henderson and Hepworth – who came to South Africa at the end of the 19th century and set themselves up in various parts of the country.

My mother received her schooling in Grahamstown, after which she took up a bookkeeping position at Holdcroft's in the main street of Benoni, until she met and married my father, Cecil John Worrall, who had been born in Woodstock, Cape Town, and, like many young people in those days, had come to Johannesburg to make his fortune on the gold mines. My father was an athlete of note. He played soccer and boxed in the late 1920s, was the South African 4-mile and 10-mile champion and was shortlisted to represent South Africa in the Amsterdam Olympics of 1928. In his later years he played tennis and golf. Although none of us achieved these heights, my two brothers and I certainly inherited his interest in and enjoyment of sport and physical exercise.

My father had a deep and abiding concern for the coloured community, and I believe that it was because he was born and bred in Woodstock. Woodstock was known at that time of high racial awareness as 'a nod-and-a-wink kind of Cape Town suburb, an easy-going place tolerant of coloured persons who were sufficiently light-skinned to "pass" as whites and to step up a station in life', according to the historian Bill Nasson. Much later I would come to understand the issues of race classification as a member of Parliament for the Gardens constituency. Most of my constituency work was involved with assisting people, in mostly sad and tragic circumstances, to have their identity changed. These came not only from Gardens but from suburbs like Woodstock, Salt River and Observatory. Many of them, whom I had managed to help, became quiet friends for years afterwards.

Although my father did well in the mines, his interest, in which he was supported by my mother, was farming. And so it was that around 1943 he cashed in his chips and bought a farm in the Cradock district in the Karoo, with the intention of settling there in the course of time. My middle brother, Terry, and I went off to boarding school in Cradock. Unfortunately, the wool boom which he had anticipated did not happen, and so my father in 1946

sold the farm and instead bought a fruit farm – mainly apricots and grapes –
in Wellington, which to this day is a pretty and unspoilt little town about an
hour's drive from Cape Town. The farm which we owned was Onverwacht,
(Unexpected) and is situated on the slopes of the mountain below the Du
Toit's Kloof Pass. My brothers and I cycled to school in Wellington.

Happy as these years were, they did not turn out well from a financial
point of view. It seems that our father had paid for more trees and vines than
there actually were on the farm. A court case followed, which my father
won. His advocate was Andrew Beyers, the larger-than-life and colourful
figure who later as judge-president pronounced Dimitri Tsafendas, Prime
Minister Hendrik Verwoerd's assassin, not guilty by virtue of insanity.

The last stage in the Worrall family's migration from Johannesburg to
Cape Town occurred when my father met a Scotsman, William Simpson,
and they together took over a road construction company. The company's
headquarters were in the northern suburbs of Cape Town and so my parents bought a house first in Boston Estate, Bellville, and then in Kenridge,
Durbanville, where we lived until my father retired to our holiday home in
Gordon's Bay. He died there in 1977 and my mother was left well-off and
enjoyed a happy widowhood until her death in 2002.

2

THE NORTHERN SUBURBS

O nce settled, my brothers and I went to Bellville Primary School, which was within walking distance of our home. It was a parallel-medium school but predominantly Afrikaans and, naturally at that time, white.

While it would not have occurred to them then, my parents' decision to settle in Bellville was a good one with some very positive consequences. Although predominantly Afrikaans-speaking, Bellville was a remarkably tolerant and open society. The member of Parliament was Jan Haak, who would be appointed as a Cabinet minister by Prime Minister John Vorster. His partner Bert Marais was our family attorney; and the mayor of Bellville was Alec Sacks, the owner of a very large hardware business. The Bellville community was also religiously and culturally diverse. We lived on the corner of 10th Avenue and Salisbury Street. Bennie Rabinowitz, who has become a dear friend, lived on the corner of 6th Avenue and Salisbury Street; and Mervyn Smith, who became a major figure in the Jewish community in Cape Town and nationally, and represented South African lawyers internationally, was at Bellville Primary School with me. For all his life Mervyn practised as an attorney in Bellville. Helen Zille has said that 'his name belongs in the pantheon of legal heroes of the new South Africa, but because he was challenging the ANC, it will take somewhat longer for his crucial contribution to democracy to be adequately acknowledged'. Temma Gad (née Weinberg) was the most popular girl in our matric class. I don't recall ever experiencing any anti-Semitism in school or in the community. In fact, what Bellville gave me, aside from a reasonably good high school education, was a sense of the richness of different cultures and, in particular, of the Afrikaans language.

Of course, tolerance and acceptance of different religions, languages and cultures, which I experienced, started in the home. My parents were Christians, my father nominally so, my mother more serious but not a regular church-goer. However, being an Irish Protestant, she wasn't always objective about Catholics. Of Jewish people, I was told from an early stage to eat the fish on my plate because the reason Jews are so clever is that they eat a lot of fish. As far as I can recall, all our family doctors down the years had been Jewish – the last one in Bellville being Leslie Levy.

Our home had books – my mother in particular was a regular reader – and a piano, which my mother played well and to which her three sons with varying degrees of enthusiasm had to apply themselves to a half-hour of 'practice' every day. Many years later in upper New York State in the cellar bar of the Delta Phi fraternity at Cornell University on an old honky-tonk piano, the girl who was to become my wife tells me I advanced my cause with a particular rendition of 'When Irish eyes are smiling'.

My schooling and teenage experience had the benefit that I only came to appreciate much later. Remember that I'm writing this over sixty-five years since I went to high school and perceptions of group relations have changed dramatically; social dynamics in our country are totally different; and there is a new national identity emerging in which white South Africans are likely to be subordinate players. But at that time, my upbringing and specifically my schooling in Bellville freed me of that 'benign superiority towards Afrikaners' which characterised white English-speakers down the years.

Aside from learning to speak Afrikaans well, something which was essential in politics and when I practised as an advocate (as most of the criminal work I did was in Afrikaans), I came to understand Afrikaners and their aspirations; and Afrikaans was the immediate language in certain friendships. For example, when together with Frederik van Zyl Slabbert, Schalk Pienaar, Adam Small, Japie Basson, Wynand Malan or FW de Klerk, we invariably spoke Afrikaans.

The critically important thing is that I learnt to understand Afrikaner views and their aspirations. Most of us have forgotten this now or adopt a 'good riddance' attitude to Afrikaner nationalism. The fact is that the political history of South Africa in the 20th century until 1984 is the story of the rise in Afrikaner nationalism and the steady but certain moulding of constitutional and political relations to suit their thinking. Whereas to

English-speaking whites, and a very powerful leader like General Smuts and even Jan Hofmeyr, the discrimination against black people and persons of colour which they introduced and enforced as policy was simply racial in kind. By contrast, the driving force behind the apartheid of Afrikaners was as much nationalism and the natural determination to grow itself as racial consciousness. In the end, the real struggle for control of South Africa would be between two indigenous nationalisms – the Afrikaner and the African.

What impressed me then, and continues to impress me, is how Afrikaners have responded to the new social and political reality. They had all the power; it was their state; and the adjustments they have had to make have been enormous. Yet they have made – and continue to make – the changes. What many of us don't remember is that it was not a simple adaptation to F.W. de Klerk's dramatic speech in February 1990, which I describe later. That speech represented the end of a whole process, an aspect of the South African situation that I know fascinates lots of people.

What of course is missing from this account is any connection with persons of colour other than in an employment capacity, which I know is difficult for any white person under the age of let's say thirty years today to grasp. And this is something I will come to.

3

MY LAST YEARS
OF SCHOOL

I was 13 years old when the 1948 election was held on 26 May and I don't remember much about it. But two things stand out in my mind. The first was how a neighbouring farmer, Mr Piet Smit (we were still living in Wellington), sounded a lorry horn every time the SABC announced a constituency win for the National Party. Whether the horn helped or not, shortly after the election Mr Piet Smit became Senator Smit. The other thing I remember was something my father said to me just after the election. I had wanted to be a Boy Scout but there wasn't an organisation in Wellington. So I suggested that perhaps I could join the Afrikaans equivalent, the Voortrekkers. My father clearly wanted to think about this, but after the election he advised against it, saying: 'We must first see what these people are going to do.'

I don't believe my parents were active members of the ruling United Party, but they strongly supported it. My father had pronounced political views. Having been brought up in the Cape and having lived in Woodstock, he never forgave the National Party for removing coloured voters from the common roll and he reacted sharply to South Africa becoming a republic. In fact, in February 1947 my parents took my brothers and me into Cape Town to watch the Royal Family's arrival.

The 1953 election was in my last year at school when I was already politically conscious – although my interest was as much in international affairs as in national politics. I tried not to miss a single one of A.M. van Schoor's weekly radio talks on foreign affairs. (Incidentally, we'd later become very good colleagues in the Senate and on the President's Council.)

But Alexander Steward's evening contributions around supper time were viewed in the Worrall household as government propaganda. I concluded much later from a slim volume of elegant essays he wrote that it was not the content of his talks so much as his insistence on reading them himself. He had a very superior, oily tone which alienated English-speaking listeners. His son, Dave Steward, a good acquaintance, who followed him into the diplomatic corps, is the person who from its creation very effectively ran F.W. de Klerk's Foundation and, as F.W. acknowledges, is almost the co-author of his memoir *The Last Trek: A New Beginning*.

The plan was that on matriculating I would go on to the University of Cape Town to study law. While my mother arranged for me to spend an hour or so with the family attorney, my father would have preferred me to study engineering and join the successful road construction company he had established. I don't think he appreciated how poor my maths was. So the decision was taken – it was to be law. Yet my preparation and reading in 1953 had a mostly political orientation.

Biography, philosophy and particularly political philosophy were the main areas of interest. I had read Plato's *Republic* and Aristotle's *Politics*, and had discovered John Stuart Mill and Edmund Burke through C.E.M. Joad in the Teach Yourself series. Incidentally, I believe that a proper understanding of the English liberal tradition includes both Mill and Burke, a point of view which has not been shared by many English-speaking South African liberals, as is evident in the pages to follow.

In the first week of the new term Professor Andrew Murray, head of the Department of Philosophy, in his capacity as Dean of the Arts Faculty, in a welcome address to new students encouraged us. 'At the end of the year you should be taking home a full trunk load of books,' I remember him saying. It was advice which I was pleased to hear but it didn't apply to me.

There was a branch of Maskew Miller near the top of Adderley Street on the left-hand side going up towards the Groote Kerk. And at the back of the shop was a tall, rather lonely stand-alone bookshelf where on the top shelf, seemingly forgotten, I found most of the volumes in the Thinker's Library series, and that's where my monthly pocket money of 10 shillings went. Charles Darwin's *Autobiography* cost two shillings and ninepence, J.S. Mill's *On Liberty* and Machiavelli's *The Prince* each cost one shilling and sixpence. Among many others, including the venerable C.E.M. Joad referred to earlier (my edition dates to 1935), these volumes sit comfortably on my bookshelves today – possibly the most travelled and prized volumes in the world, having followed every step in my career.

One further aspect of interest at this time in my life was a relationship which I developed with the Rev. Alan Dennis Dietrich, who was the minister of the Bellville Presbyterian Church. He was an old bachelor and quite a remarkable man. For example, he won a *Cape Argus* cooking competition in which the competitors were required to design a Christmas lunch for six people within a certain cost. He was also intensely involved with the moral reform of people in jail. Although I am today not a church-going person, there is an important sense in which I am religious, and it was as theological adviser that I got to know Dietrich well. He lent me theological books and we had some interesting discussions. As a result I knew how a sermon was structured and actually put this to practice in three sermons – two in the Bellville Church and one in the beautiful Presbyterian Church in Woodstock, which is still in use. Many years later I found among some papers my father's baptismal certificate. It is dated 25 August 1909 and the place of baptism was the Woodstock Presbyterian Church.

I suppose among the high points at school were that I was headboy – an English speaker in a predominantly Afrikaans school – senior cadet officer, played first-team cricket and first-team rugby, and was one-mile champion of the co-ed schools. What should be clear is that the school syllabus didn't figure. In fact, the only part of my high school career, which was otherwise totally undistinguished from an academic point of view, in which I achieved some recognition was debating. I won the Abe Bailey national prize for bilingualism and was judged the best speaker in the school for two years running. I tutored myself with Dale Carnegie's *Public Speaking and Influencing Men in Business*: my well-worn copy is dated 1945.

All my teachers have passed on, with the exception of Mrs May Rabinowitz (née Lahee), who taught me English and who at 99 years is a frequent and delightful Sunday lunch companion with Anita and me at Bennie Rabinowitz's La Perla table. I have nothing but praise and thanks to those men and women who did their best to encourage and reward my efforts at learning. They should be praised while they are still around – something which I think we managed to convey to our three sons.

4

START OF UNIVERSITY

Having matriculated in 1953 I went on to the University of Cape Town where I spent the better part of five years. Aside from the many long-standing friendships I made and intellectual interests I developed, these were very formative and happy years – and I am referring to the whole UCT experience: the academic studies, some remarkable teachers, the student politics, and extramural activities (debating and the Philosophical Society) and sport (I played rugby for third team and won a blue for cross-country), and the novelty and delight in meeting persons of colour whom I got to know and respect and whose friendship continued beyond university.

Among the teachers whom I remember with respect and fondness were Andrew Murray, Martin Versfeld, Sim du Plessis, Jack Simons, Denis Cowen, Ben Beinart and Wouter de Vos. Jeremy Lawrence, the writer, tells of being in one of Jack Simons's classes and mentions me in this context: 'The questioning of my maverick fellow-student Denis Worrall was a lively feature of our classes.' Simons was par excellence the campus communist, but we liked him very much, with his sardonic sense of humour, corduroy jacket, red tie and red socks – always a talking point. He was later stupidly served with a banning order which regrettably prevented him from teaching.

My initiation into student politics came in the first week, when I was the prime mover of a motion at the freshers' debate. Chairing the debate was John Didcott, who at the time was president of the SRC and who would go on to have a stellar legal career and, notwithstanding his strong liberal credentials and opposition to apartheid, would be appointed a judge by the National Party government. A facilitator in the debate was the irrepressible Ernie Wentzel, who died early, leaving a very feisty wife, Jill, to continue in his place. Two of the speakers were Fred Stander, a very clever Afrikaans law student who just loved stirring the pot, and Ian Farlam, who had the ability to see and exploit the funny side of most things and who was later to distinguish himself as a judge. These two were stalwarts of the debating society, both of them winning the best speaker award.

A year later I was elected to the Day Students Council and shortly afterwards to the Student Representative Council. In 1957 I was elected vice-chairman, having polled the second highest votes. Neville Rubin, who was a year ahead of me and who had a brilliant career in international student affairs, was president and for much of the term was overseas on a bursary. I then acted as president. The main issue in student politics was concern with government plans to introduce statutory university apartheid and the threat, therefore, to academic freedom and university autonomy which this could entail.

At this time I did a lot of writing and speaking on these issues. Greatly encouraged by Colin Eglin and Zach de Beer, I joined the United Party, which was of course the main opposition party in Parliament and was subsequently elected chairman of the Cape Peninsula Youth Council. Eglin was chairman of the senior body on which I was also a member. In his memoir, *Crossing the Borders of Power*, he refers to the long and close relationship we had together which began at that time. I met many other leading politicians who had actually served in the Smuts government – people like Harry Lawrence, Hamilton Russell, Sidney Waterson, and Piet van der Byl. I did not meet Advocate J.G.N. Strauss, who was then UP leader, but got to know his successor, Sir de Villiers Graaff, very well and came to respect him highly when he took over the leadership in 1956.

In 1954, when I went to university, the English-language universities, Cape Town and the University of Witwatersrand in particular, were in a state of turmoil – a turmoil which reflected the power of the conflicting emotions generated by the two watershed elections of May 1948 and April 1953. Most accounts of apartheid as a concept and policy identify the 1948 election as the point at which it was introduced. This is correct, but the 1953 election is in a way more significant. The National Party's victory in 1948 came as an enormous surprise to the United Party and its supporters and even to the NP. It was almost seen as something of an accident; and indeed the election statistics show the NP won with a minority of votes owing to the nature of the electoral system and delimitation. Among UP supporters and

English-speakers in general, there was a very real expectation that the tide would turn with the 1953 election. It didn't happen, and what the 1953 election instead suggested was that the country was in for a long period of Afrikaner rule. This was confirmed by the 1958 election, when the NP increased its percentage of votes to more than 55%.

These two elections had a bearing on my personal views and my political thinking down the years. Firstly, formal South African politics (the political party system and institutions of government) until around 1985 were 'whites only' politics, and the major political parties promoted race discrimination in some form or other – whether it was called 'segregation' or 'apartheid', the principle was the same: discrimination in various forms against persons of colour and black South Africans in particular, to the advantage of white South Africans.

To illustrate the point, the UP government in 1946 – in other words, two years before the NP came to power – introduced legislation restricting the right of the Asian community to acquire property in certain areas of Natal and the Transvaal. General Smuts, as Prime Minister, in justifying the measure, spoke of 'Durban being a European city and would remain one'. This led to the government of India referring the treatment of persons of Indo-Pakistani descent in South Africa to the UN General Assembly in 1946.

Secondly, these elections created a leadership crisis in opposition politics and especially within the English-speaking intelligentsia. The death in December 1948 of Jan Hofmeyr, who was regarded especially by the English-speaking intelligentsia as a natural successor to Smuts, and the death of Smuts shortly afterwards, came as a tremendous shock to thinking English speakers. Hofmeyr never offered a consistent position on race relations but his public statements suggested that, given the opportunity, he would go much further than Smuts in creating a more racially inclusive society. And it is hard to exaggerate the importance of the 'Oubaas', as he was affectionately known to English-speaking South Africans. His reputation stretched across the world. (One wonders how many young South Africans know that two of the four statues outside Westminster in London are South Africans – Smuts and Nelson Mandela. The other two are Abraham Lincoln and Winston Churchill.)

The point I am making is that when I commenced studies at UCT in 1954, racial separation was and had been an integral part of the political system and the country's politics from its inception. To illustrate the point differently, Helen Suzman, whose career of thirty-six years in Parliament is universally and quite rightly celebrated, was first elected to Parliament in 1948 on a segregation ticket, and once on her party's slogan of 'white leadership with justice'. Segregation was the governing principle of relations between the races even though there were individual white South Africans who before 1948 and the NP's victory pleaded for an inclusive political system – persons like Margaret Ballinger, Edgar Brookes, Donald Molteno, Leslie Rubin, Oscar Wollheim, Sam Kahn, Alan Paton and Leo Marquard, to mention a few.

However, until after the 1953 election, when three months later they were involved in establishing the Liberal Party, these notables would have voted UP. There was no other choice. This point is very clearly illustrated by Colin Eglin's experience. He explains in detail how he was pressured into joining the Liberal Party but resisted because he believed the UP was a more effective option. It was a decision Colin says which caused him great anguish. This is perfectly understandable. Philosophically he was with them. But he knew that power, even relatively speaking, was with the UP. This was the central dilemma experienced by many whites, English- and Afrikaans-speakers, since the establishment of the Union but critically after 1948. Over the long term I suppose one could say that Alan Paton personified it on the English-speaking side and on the Afrikaans side the philosopher and poet N.P. van Wyk Louw, who expressed it in his idea of *liberale nasionalisme*.

5

SALUTING FRIENDSHIP

I made many friendships at the University of Cape Town but one stands out: Adam Small, the philosopher, poet and dramatist. Adam, who passed away in June 2016, and I were the same age when we began our studies on the same day at the University of Cape Town. Adam concentrated on philosophy, language and literature. I tried to combine as much philosophy with the compulsory undergraduate law subjects as possible.

The result is that we got to know each other from the very first year and, on graduating, we independently chose to do the honours course in philosophy. Being the only students in that year, we had our classes together and got to know each other and our teachers extremely well. Professor Murray was the political philosopher; Dr Martin Versfeld, the eminent Thomist scholar, taught us ethics; and Sim du Plessis, a product of the University of the Orange Free State, taught us logic. Versfeld and Du Plessis adopted different philosophical positions and had running debates which happily involved the two of us right down to personal issues: I remember Du Plessis once telling us in a particular argument, 'You should see the state of Martin's fishing tackle-bag!'

Knowing Adam from the very beginning of my university days has been a great experience and honour, and it has been an enormous pleasure watching him make the great contribution which he has made to the academic and intellectual life of this country. His contribution goes way beyond philosophy. He's made his mark in poetry, in literature and the theatre, and I am very proud to be called his friend – and was therefore naturally surprised but delighted by his publication in the *Cape Times* on 22 October 2015 of his 'Saluting Friendship' poem, which follows.

6

'A Tribute to the Two of Us: Dr Denis Worrall, in Friendship', by Adam Small

We were so young. They taught us philosophy at UCT – Martin Versfeld, Andrew Murray and Sim du Plessis. We worked concertedly, our search for wisdom emblazoned by the memory of ancient Athens: the Parthenon on the Acropolis, and the Areopagus where we were told Socrates consorted with kindred spirits, young and old.

On an afternoon, years later, I sat, my back against one of the fluted pillars of the great monument, and saw red poppies beautifully grow around that architecture of eternity – and I understood how right the great poet Bashu was to say that flowers should rather not be picked but left intact simply for us to marvel at.

Now, deep in our years, there is a story worth to tell: of two young men – boys we were really still – climbing the many steps at UCT; to and from classes, talking in between, about engaging concepts.

We embraced the life of intellect avidly and self-assured.

We were still so young!

We dreamt great dreams.

We advanced to maturity over ground at times quite smooth, at times uneven and rough and floundered often, though never fell and finally reached heights from which we now can look out far upon realities achieved, from which we need not hide: indeed, which we can show the world with pride.

As time passed, we've been taken by Jana Beranova's words: 'If no one listens to no one, there will be a failing unto death instead of an exchange of words.'

You and I, thoughtfully, however over time have learned to listen to each other, and to others.

So, let us drink a toast and think: our day, at last, will be. But it does not matter really, for we can smile, happy and joyously, knowing that we have ordered our existence so that, finally, we can say: we have not striven to no end, not lived in vain …

7

THE USA, GHANA AND NIGERIA

At the end of 1959, when I had completed my master's degree and most of the LLB at the University of Cape Town, I accepted a lectureship in political science at the University of South Africa. I had hoped this would be of short duration as I very much wanted to study overseas. I had been one of three finalists for the Cape Rhodes scholarship in 1959. The other candidates were Norman Bromberger, a brilliant economist and a prominent UCT student leader, and a Rhodes University student, who was the successful candidate. Norman subsequently received a UCT scholarship which took him to Oxford, and through the American Embassy I was awarded the equivalent of a Fulbright scholarship by the Institute of International Education in New York, which covered travel and academic costs.

The question was: which university should I apply to? My list of preferences was made up of Ivy League universities – Yale, Princeton, Harvard and Cornell, which is in upper New York State. Cornell came through very quickly with the offer of an assistantship in the Department of Political Science, I think partly because I had met Professor Clinton Rossiter, Cornell's head of the Government Department and one of America's top scholars on the US presidency, during a visit he made to South Africa the previous year. The result was that I left South Africa in August for New York via London – which was my first trip overseas.

My arrival in what was in those days Idlewild Airport and my first days in that great city were bewildering to say the least. I arrived in Manhattan around midnight. There was a commuter strike and for some reason the reservation made for me at the Taft Hotel was not registered and most hotels were fully booked. So I left my luggage at the Taft, which is just off Times Square, and spent much of the night exploring the famous square. At one point I was approached by two attractive young ladies, one of whom adroitly put a hand where it pleases most and said: 'Honey, why so saft?' Just at that moment, a cab pulled up, the back door opened and a gentleman invited them to join him.

My first call that morning was to the Institute of International Education, which rescheduled my flight to Ithaca and Cornell to late that afternoon. The president of the IIE was Louise Woods, wife of George Woods, himself president of the World Bank, who was amused by my account of the night's activities and invited me to their apartment where after a shave and shower and a very enjoyable lunch she sent me off to the airport. I tell this because aside from the fact that shortly afterwards and for the duration of my stay in America I received high-level World Bank reports and documents, I also received an invitation to consider working for the Bank.

At the time Norman and I were hoping to study overseas, there was an intense debate as to which was the more beneficial option from a South African student's point of view. Did Oxford and Cambridge, for example, offer a more fulfilling graduate education than one of the better American universities? There was no doubt in my mind that for me Cornell was the better option. Had I gone to Oxford, I would have chosen a subject with my supervisor's approval, started reading and researching it, returning every now and again to report back to him or her, and finally writing it up.

In an American doctoral programme the candidate would first have to complete several courses of study in his or her field (in my case political science), generally taking three years to do so before starting on the dissertation. While this usually extended the time required for a PhD, it certainly ensured an altogether more thorough education at the postgraduate level.

To illustrate, between my registration at Cornell and when my dissertation topic was confirmed, I had completed and passed examinations in selected courses in American government, political theory, international relations, and comparative government. In this way I think I filled a lot of gaps in my South African education and developed many new perspectives within my field of study.

Associated with the courses, and reinforcing them, was my role as a teaching assistant to distinguished scholars like Allan Bloom, Clinton Rossiter,

Andrew Hacker and Steven Muller, chairman of my doctoral committee, who went on to achieve the distinction of being President of Johns Hopkins University from 1972 to 1990. But my most famous teacher at Cornell was probably Allan Bloom, the author of the 1987 bestselling *The Closing of the American Mind*, which he followed up with a brilliant book on literature called *Giants and Dwarfs*.

The fact is Cornell was more than just an academic experience. My stellar colleagues introduced me to the American intellectual scene and specifically to the New York intellectual community. It was indirectly through my teachers that I could call Norman Podhoretz, editor of *Commentary*, the most serious American Jewish publication, Irving Kristol, Midge Decter, Kevin Phillips, William Buckley, and the people at *National Review* and *New Republic* as friends. I had lunch with Irving Kristol almost every time I went to New York. And on one visit to William Buckley he suggested using his car to take me back to the hotel – an offer I accepted. It turned out to be a chauffeur-driven Cadillac which I shared with the family poodle.

* * *

The 20th century is widely regarded as the American century, and I'm immensely grateful to have had a small living experience of this great country, its people, cultures, institutions and as a field of ideas. The highlights of my time there included experiencing at first hand the assassination of JFK; the Cuban missile crisis; the space race; much of the Civil Rights Movement; the emergence of Malcolm X and Black Power; the freedom rides; and the start of the Vietnam war.

I was also privileged to be in the US during a period of transformation in social thought when fundamental concepts and principles of American government would be challenged. There was not a political science faculty in any major university at the time which was not confronted by these issues and often strongly divided. The American political system had never fully reflected the democratic principles – particularly of political equality – which the founding fathers had introduced into it.

During the 1960s, groups that previously had been submerged began more forcefully, but with varying degrees of success, to promote themselves. These included African Americans, Native Americans, and women. Much of the support they received came from a generation younger and larger than ever before, making its way through a college and university system that was expanding at an ever-rapid rate.

* * *

The US offered me a very broad canvas of interest from a research point of view, but there were four areas of particular interest to me personally – both as a scholar and as a South African. The first was obviously the Civil Rights Campaign. The 1950s saw a rise in racial awareness and the first of several major desegregation measures, namely *Brown* versus *Board of Education*, which in 1954 declared segregation in schools to be unconstitutional. Closely related to this was the issue of political leadership and its management of change at a time of convulsive social and economic transformation. The third area turned on the argument around the nature of American society – was it mainly constituted of groups and communities or individuals? And how were their distinctive interests to be coordinated? As thoughtful South Africans will recognise, this was then and is still a fundamental unresolved issue in our own country.

And, fourthly, I was interested in American interest in emerging Africa – both from a political and an economic point of view. From an early point in my stay in America, I familiarised myself with the race relations situation academically and in a practical way by participating in organised study groups to the South – notably Mississippi and Alabama. These trips made two strong impressions on me. The first was just how ubiquitous segregation was; and, secondly, the arrogance of Northerners towards Southern liberals who were working to change the situation – especially given what was clear, that the problem was not simply a Southern one. Country club discrimination was widespread in the north as was evident in the Rotary clubs I was invited to address and even Ithaca, where Cornell is situated, had its significant African-American suburb, which students only visited for cheap beer and sex. At another level, as academic adviser to the Delta Phi Fraternity at Cornell I could not persuade them at 'rushing time' that they should identify and invite one or two African Americans to be brothers. It remained all white.

What was also clear was that at a national level policy and practice were falling behind Civil Rights rhetoric. Good examples were the Civil Rights Act of 1964, which outlawed discrimination in all public accommodation, and in the next year the Voting Rights Act, which authorised the Federal government to register voters where state and local authorities prevented African Americans from doing so. This legislation was locked in Congress. Here leadership became critical – an issue which fascinated me.

As regards leadership, there were two dominant leaders during the period I was in the United States – John Fitzgerald Kennedy (JFK) and Lyndon Baines Johnson (LBJ.) They had very different styles which I believe reflected their social backgrounds. Kennedy was born into a rich, politically connected Boston family of Irish Catholics. He was one of nine siblings with a privileged childhood of elite schools, Harvard University, sailboats, servants, summer homes, and travel abroad. Indeed, Kennedy with his elegant and beautiful wife, Jacqueline, almost spun a reality out of the Camelot myth which the media created around them. One would therefore expect of JFK to be independent-minded; to have an adventurous and risk-taking approach to life; be very self-assured and confident; careless of ruling social norms; and intellectually arrogant.

LBJ, by contrast, was born in Stonewall, Texas, in a small farmhouse, the eldest of five children. He was raised as a Baptist and, after doing odd jobs in California on a borrowed $75, he enrolled in a teachers' college and on graduation took a job teaching public speaking. Later, as a politician LBJ was influenced into adopting strong positive attitudes towards Jews by the religious beliefs that his family, especially his grandfather, shared with him. Given LBJ's widely acknowledged ability and powers of persuasion, it doesn't come as a surprise that his favourite Bible reading came from Isaiah: 'Come now, and let us reason together.'

In LBJ's temperament one would expect a sensitivity to others; an appreciation of hard work; striving for betterment; a consciousness of social and economic circumstances; a promoter of commitment to self-improvement; and a strong empathy for those less fortunate. For this reason the concept of the Great Society was more LBJ's than Kennedy's. Like Johnson, Kennedy had been a Senator. But, unlike Johnson, who was a Senator's Senator, he had never become part of the Congress.

So it was Johnson who, after Kennedy's assassination, when feelings were still raw, persuaded the Senate to give up delaying tactics and pass the civil rights legislation, including the Voting Act. To this day I have a vivid memory of that speech. It was his first speech to both chambers as president, and the speech had been written by Ted Sorensen, Kennedy's speechwriter

– something which was very evident: it wasn't LBJ's style. But at a certain point in delivering it, LBJ paused, looked up at the gallery, and in the thickest of Southern accents said: 'Ah bin in Congress for 25 years. And ah got Congress in the marrow o' my bones.' The response was electric. They were all the way with LBJ.

I suspect that, given his background, LBJ's liberal idealism was much deeper than that of JFK. But my respect for him also relates to his lack of pretence, his sense of doing what was right – whatever the cost. He was a Southern politician through and through and never pretended to be anything else. And yet he had the moral courage (after telling the truth, I believe, the most important ethical value in a politician) to take a stance which was contrary to his own political interests. There's a famous speech that Johnson made that epitomises this. In October 1964 in New Orleans he told of an old Southern Senator who said that before he died he wanted the people of Louisiana to hear one genuine Democratic speech because 'all that I ever hear at election time is Negra, Negra, Negra'. The reports are that, combined with Johnson's personal identification, the speech received an enormous ovation after the initial shock caused by the President's language had subsided. As somebody remarked, this speech highlights Johnson's persuasive powers at their best – frank, heartfelt and a little earthy.

Many people regard LBJ's speech on the passing of the Voting Rights Act as his greatest oratorical triumph. That speech ended with: 'Because it's not just Negroes, but all of us, who must overcome the legacy of bigotry and injustice.' He paused dramatically for several seconds, then adopting the lyrics of the Civil Rights Movement, he stated forcefully: 'And we shall overcome!' It is at this point Johnson is said to have remarked quietly to his young White House assistant Bill Moyers: 'Bill, I think we have just delivered the South to the Republican Party for a long time to come' – a prediction I am pleased to say turned out to be wrong.

President Kennedy was the first in 1961 to use the term 'affirmative action' as a way of redressing the disadvantages of discrimination that had persisted. But it was a concept developed and reinforced for the first time by Lyndon Johnson. As he put it: 'This is the next and the more profound stage in the battle for Civil Rights. We will not just seek equality as a right and a theory, but equality as a fact with actual results.' What should be very evident is that I admired Lyndon Johnson enormously; and although I never met him, I learnt a great deal from him during my stay in America.

* * *

The Civil Rights Movement in the 1960s raised a number of very important issues relating to the American economy, education, political participation, and the social structure of the society. But as important as many of these was the nature of American society. Was it a society of individuals, as the founding fathers assumed and the Constitution instructed? Or was it a society of communities *and* individuals? And how were they to relate in terms of policy priorities? Suddenly in the 1960s this became a key point of debate in intellectual circles and in American universities.

The widely accepted view until then was that the US was a country of immigrants, and as new waves of immigrants came, they melted into the existing American nation. This was a fundamental concept in thinking about the political and social foundations of the nation and in public policy. Suddenly, in 1963 two highly reputable scholars – Nathan Glazer and Daniel Moynihan – with the publication of their book *Beyond the Melting Pot* put this cardinal concept into doubt.

Their researches had shown that the children and grandchildren of earlier immigrants to New York City had retained their ethnic consciousness and therefore that the phenomenon of persistent ethnic identities over the course of generations would continue. These findings obviously had immense implications for the increasingly dominant African American Civil Rights Movement. Stopping the integration of African Americans as individuals did not seem to be the answer. Yes, desegregation had to happen – social and economic backgrounds caused by centuries of political inequality had to be compensated for by group-based affirmative programmes and actions. These would involve racial preferences and quotas, and when applied in, for example, educational institutions, they raised all sorts of questions. How would this affect academic standards? How would it affect university autonomy? And how would quotas affect groups who were possibly overly represented in America's best universities – for example, Jewish Americans?

An intense debate followed specifically around the issue of quotas until the US Supreme Court in a landmark decision in 1978 ruled that affirmative action was constitutional but the court invalidated the use of racial quotas. These issues were obviously of enormous interest to me as a South African. They certainly impacted on political science and practice. We have yet to find answers to the thorny question of how one reconciles a commitment to individual liberty and rights with the rights and interest of groups.

* * *

It surprised me when I arrived at Cornell that there was not a single African specialist in the Department of Politics. It had specialists in every other region of the world but nothing on Africa. This was widely the case at American universities at that time, but it was to change dramatically as a result of the establishment in 1953 of the African American Institute in Washington. Supported by three foundations – Carnegie, Ford and Rockefeller – it was a significant funder of research and of American academic initiatives in Africa.

Ghana, of course, became independent in 1957 with the promise of many African countries to follow. In fact, 1960 saw 17 countries becoming independent, with Zimbabwe the 41st in 1981. African independence was followed in the US in the 1960s with immense pride and optimism. The general sentiment, especially among academics and church people was, as one leading commentator put it, 'that the Africans were creating a wonderful new world, a sort of new humanism'. Scholarly involvement followed, with Gwendolen Carter leading the pack in 1958 with her ground-breaking *South Africa: The Politics of Inequality – Politics in South Africa since 1948*. James Coleman and others were to follow shortly afterwards.

That this heavy optimism was to end in profound disappointment is not part of my story. But it was against this background that Professor Muller and the faculty at Cornell supported my decision to devote my dissertation to Nigeria, which had become independent in 1960. I spent the better part of the academic year at the University of Ibadan in Eastern Nigeria.

My interest stemmed specifically from the fact that Nigeria, which like South Africa is culturally and ethnically very diverse, adopted federalism in response to its diversity. The country was launched with a constitution corresponding more or less to the three major groupings. Today it has 36 states, most of them with a cultural or ethnic core. One reason I chose to research Nigeria was to determine the applicability of federalism to South Africa, given the Nigerian experience.

I decided that en route to Lagos I would spend some time in Ghana which became independent in 1957. But there was a problem in that Ghana required South Africans (I presume only white South Africans) to sign a declaration of opposition to apartheid as a condition for being issued a visa. As I did not want to create political problems for myself on my return to South Africa, I went to the South African Embassy in Rome, which on my flight was the last stop-off point in Europe before Accra, naively hoping to see the Ambassador and explain that I was a student on his way to do research in Nigeria and it would be silly not to take advantage of this opportunity of visiting the first of the African countries to become independent. The Ambassador was not available to see me but the minister did. I recall his name was Gelderblom and he had a habit of raising his eyebrows as he spoke. This time he raised one eyebrow very high when he asked me: 'You, of course, know what Dr Verwoerd would say?' Yes, but this was an opportunity I could not miss. I was going – and I did go – and when I got to know Dr Verwoerd much later, I have absolutely no doubt that he would've said: 'Young man, you must go!' But obviously this is just by the way.

During the eight days I was in Accra, I spoke with several journalists, some members of Parliament, and notably the secretary-general of the powerful Trade Union Council, N.A. Welbeck, who was also one of Kwame Nkrumah's closest aides. To his enormous credit he agreed to me sitting in his office for a day in an observer capacity, and while there I had an experience of where Ghana was going politically. Apparently, a by-election was being organised and Welbeck received a call advising him that some unauthorised person wanted to stand. 'Cancel the election!' was Welbeck's curt instruction. Shortly afterwards, in fact in 1964, the constitution was changed to make Ghana a one-party state and Nkrumah's Convention People's Party was declared the only legal party – so setting a major political precedent in emerging Africa.

On arrival at Lagos airport I had my first experience of a mammy wagon – that colourful, popular vehicle of transportation of both humans and small animals all over West Africa – which delivered me to the University of Ibadan some one hundred miles to the east of Lagos. And there I was accommodated in the Amadou Bello residence as an ordinary student. No concessions were asked for and none were offered. And unlike two German researchers who had a special European diet, I had what the students ate and in fact came to like the diet very much.

As far as social drinking is concerned, it was Star beer, now and again mixed with palm wine. A weekend pleasure was to go to the now famous Mbari Mbayo art and literary club, where the Lebanese owner-chef prepared the most delicious roast chicken with West African jazz in the background.

The only time I had wine during my stay was at diplomatic functions – with my German friends, I was a regular at the British, German and Austrian embassies. The Austrian Ambassador, Wolfgang Jungwirth, was something of a scholar and took an interest in my research – and I in his pretty daughter.

The Department of Political Science consisted mainly of Ken Post, who wrote a very good book on Nigeria's first election, and Father James O'Connell, who invited me to lead tutorials and give occasional lectures. As far as the dissertation was concerned, I had done most of the historical research before coming to Nigeria – although the university library had a good collection of the official British colonial reports and papers.

My main focus was on the developing situation in Nigeria, which meant reading five daily newspapers and observing the developing political situation, which was critical as two major upsets occurred during my sojourn in Nigeria. From the beginning of independence the country's ethnic and demographic distribution had been a serious problem. The other crisis, which was related, was the breakdown of government in the Western region.

Aside from the university being excellent from a research point of view, it had all the benefits of, for example, an advanced South African university. I played a lot of squash with lecturers mainly in the Department of English; and as I had been awarded a blue at UCT for cross-country running, I took it up again – finding myself winning the mile at the Nigerian universities athletics championship and being selected to represent Nigeria in the annual Nigeria–Ghana event. When Dr Kenneth Dike, the Vice-Chancellor, awarded me my certificate, he remarked on the fact that I was the only white participating. I quipped: 'Someone has to carry the white man's burden' – a remark taken in good grace. One thing I must stress: at no time did I act as anything other than a South African, and at no time did I experience anything but friendliness.

Nigerian men have the custom when walking together to hold hands. Although it was not a custom I was familiar with, I often found myself hand-in-hand with Nigerian friends – a custom I also experienced with West Africans on my return to Cornell.

I returned to Cornell to complete writing up my dissertation after a brief but very welcome visit home to Cape Town and my family. During the visit I bumped into Sir de Villiers Graaff, leader of the United Party, the official opposition in Parliament and an old friend. His reaction to asking me what I was doing with myself, and my telling him 'studying Nigerian federalism', was: 'My dear boy, there is only one kind of federalism and that is race federalism.' This was of course the UP's counter at the time to Dr Verwoerd's so-called grand apartheid.

My last eighteen months in the US were exciting and, with my doctoral exams behind me and only the completion of the dissertation still required for my degree, unpressured and happy. The department had appointed me as a senior instructor and I was able to rent a better apartment and buy a car – a 1954 Ford. In January 1964 I met a beautiful and clever woman called Anita Denise Ianco, who was doing a PhD in psychology. Romanian by birth, she had a remarkable lineage, having lived under communist rule in Romania, and subsequently in Israel, Cuba and Canada. We found we had mutual interests.

Meanwhile, there was a close relationship between the departments of political science at UCLA and Cornell, and UCLA asked Cornell to suggest somebody who could teach comparative government for the Summer School in 1964 at an assistant professorship level. Steven Muller nominated me. His advice: 'Get yourself a girlfriend with a convertible and enjoy yourself!' And so it was that my Ford took me and three undergraduates who were returning home for the vacation, and who naturally contributed to the travel costs, from New York cross-country via Chicago and Las Vegas to Los Angeles and subsequently San Francisco. On the return trip I swung through the South up to New York, on the way giving lunch-time talks to Rotary and other clubs. Interest in South Africa and Africa was quite remarkable.

Aside from the fact that the UCLA political faculty was very impressive, with well-developed interests in Africa, I had the opportunity of getting to know Professor Ned Munger, who was one of the first American academics to start researching South Africa seriously. He was the person who described Stellenbosch University as the Princeton of South Africa. I also reconnected at UCLA with the historian Leonard Thompson, who had been Professor of History at UCT when I was a student there. And I had the privilege of meeting James Coleman, who had distinguished himself with his writings on Nigeria.

Shortly after returning to Cornell I received an offer of an assistant professorship from Kenyon College in Ohio, one of the oldest and most prestigious private colleges in the US. I reluctantly turned it down because they wanted me to commit for four years, whereas I wanted to return to South Africa and was agreeable to only two. A couple of months later I accepted an appointment as a lecturer in political science to what was then the University of Natal, Durban.

So it was that in February 1965 I returned to South Africa. My relationship with Anita had developed and blossomed and I was sorry to leave her behind. But South Africa at that time was not the most inviting place and, given my commitment to the country, I was not sure whether she would fit into South Africa. In any event, she was in the middle of her PhD and had her own career to think about. We parted at Idlewild airport, I to South Africa and she to Canada. Our sole communication until we met again in July was by airmail.

RETURN TO SOUTH AFRICA

After nearly five years away from South Africa, I returned home at the beginning of 1965 to Durban and the University of Natal (as it was then called) with no idea of how challenging the homecoming would be. I had changed, the country had changed, and only now when I look back on the two years I spent in Natal (now KZN) do I realise how important that period was.

Firstly, I needed to start developing a career and establishing myself in my chosen field of political science. This obviously meant extending what I had learnt in America and applying it in the South African context. This also meant adjusting to South African students and their methods of learning, and seeking out for myself areas of research and publishing and reaching out to fellow political scientists.

Secondly, when I left South Africa I had already developed political ambitions. After five years of political dormancy I quickly found myself assessing the political situation and wanting to familiarise myself with per-sonalities, both politically active and peripheral to politics – journalists, civic leaders and major business players across the spectrum. This was therefore a time when I had to think seriously and deeply about my own basic values and their application to the South African situation and what role I person-ally could play from a professional and a civic point of view.

I took up the appointment as a lecturer in political science at the University of Natal in January 1965, and in April I invited Anita to join me with the intention of us marrying. She accepted and, when one thinks about it, it was a very brave decision – given her family circumstances (the only daughter, deeply and proudly loved by everybody), the foreignness of South Africa, and its appalling international reputation especially in Canada. By then the country had also left the Commonwealth and was annually excoriated at the UN and other international agencies.

Anita arrived in Johannesburg where I met her before proceeding to Durban. Although I had vaguely hoped she would first see whether she could happily adjust to the country, we were married within a month of her arrival ('I am not here on appro!'). The wedding took place in Somerset West (very close to Cape Town) and my father drove her to the church and gave her away, which he did with some reservation. 'Denis, are you sure this is right?' 'Yes, Dad. Just do it!'

In any event he and my mother already loved her. The reception was at the family home in Gordon's Bay and afterwards she phoned her mother in Montréal. I think what greatly helped Anita settle in was that on our return to Durban she was immediately welcomed by Professor Ronald Albino, a truly friendly and sophisticated man and head of the psychology department and he invited Anita to join the department in a teaching capacity. In fact, the two years we spent in Durban before moving to Pretoria were two very happy years.

The most important challenge to me on returning home was to learn how to be a good husband. And after 53 years it seems the foundation laid in those two years was a solid one.

9

NATAL

W hen I left South Africa in 1961 I had a reasonable idea of what the different political parties stood for, but I didn't have any personal commitment in respect of the situation. What I took with me was a concern about the South African situation and a constant sensitivity to possible answers. It was a sensitivity I carried into my studies and into my experience in the US and Nigeria. It was an interest that was imbued with something the great 20th-century historian Arnold Toynbee once said: 'South Africa is important to the whole world – because if it can find answers as to how its different races, languages and religions can live together in peace, nobody in the world can claim to fail.' I believed in this statement of his and must have quoted it in hundreds of speeches and articles I wrote.

My interest from abroad in what was happening in South Africa was evident in my relations with our diplomatic representatives in New York and Washington. But it was manifested very directly in a letter I wrote while still at Cornell University to the South African Foreign Minister, Dr Hilgard Muller. I hadn't met Dr Muller at that time but I knew him to be a classicist and a Rhodes scholar who had completed a doctorate in law at Oxford. My letter is dated 9 June 1964 and reads:

'Dear Dr Muller, I am a lecturer in the Department of Government at Cornell University and would like to tell you that I think your exposition of government policy as reported in the *New York Times* yesterday was really good. More statements like that are needed. After a year of research in Nigeria and three years in this country, I think I have developed some idea of how our policies should be put across. Three essentials in my opinion are:

'1. That the problem be formulated in terms of a conflict of nationalisms and that the terms 'black' and 'white' be dropped altogether;

'2. That the designation 'separate development' – it has a horribly sinister ring about it – be discarded for 'territorial separation' or 'creative withdrawal' or 'partition', which is my preference. 'Segregation' must be avoided like the plague;

'3. That the emphasis in policy statements switch from socio-economic benefits to constitutional goals. The possibility, indeed probability, of independence for the Homelands, must be stressed. I realise in making these points I do not have that extra dimension – domestic politics – to take into account, but then I think it is high time that government spokesmen in South Africa take a few calculated risks with the electorate.

'Enclosed is the January issue of *The Trojan Horse*, the leading literary publication at Cornell, which carries an article by me.

'Sincerely Denis Worrall'

Some three weeks later, Dr Muller personally replied in a letter which was about four times the length of mine and dealt directly with all the points I had made. Offering something of the flavour of his letter, the opening paragraph reads:

'I would like to thank you for your letter of the 9th June, the interest you take in South African affairs, your interesting and useful suggestions, and the January issue of *The Trojan Horse* with your article on South Africa. I found several of the thoughts you develop, most stimulating. For instance, that the problem should be seen as a conflict of nationalisms, and that the emphasis should be on constitutional goals rather than on material benefits. You will find an indication of the line of my own thinking in the enclosed copies of speeches I made in London. [He was previously South African Ambassador in London.] My own experience has been that local politics need not be an obstacle to the approach you suggest, because the South African electorate is more realistic and advanced in their views than people realise. I was particularly interested in the way in which you deal with the objections and criticisms of certain aspects of our policy. Most of us admit we do not know all the answers, and we have made many mistakes and, as fallible human beings, we are bound to make many more, but we are faced with the most complex problem and are seriously trying to find a solution which will be practical as well as just to all our population groups.'

On my return to South Africa I was to link up with Dr Muller from my position at Durban and later at Unisa. Anita recalls that after she had joined me in Pretoria, where we lived, at a dinner at the Israeli Embassy at which Dr Muller was the guest of honour, he afterwards interpreted to the other guests a showcase of ancient artefacts, to the surprise also of our host, Ambassador Michaels.

In the same spirit that I had approached Foreign Minister Muller, on my return to South Africa I began to identify persons I wanted to meet and from whom I could get a better grasp of where the country was going and what their hopes and concerns were. So it was that, aside from local city and provincial officials, I wrote to several national figures among whom were Prime Minister Dr Hendrik Verwoerd, Minister of Justice John Vorster and Harry Oppenheimer of Anglo American. My opening paragraph introducing myself was the same to all three. It read: 'Since February of this year I have been lecturing in political science at UND. Prior to that I spent four years abroad, three in the US studying for a PhD and lecturing at Cornell and UCLA and one in Nigeria doing research.' All three accepted and agreed to meet me on the dates I suggested.

I met Mr Oppenheimer at his elegant office in 44 Main Street and, after a brief discussion, he invited me to lunch at a nearby restaurant, the name of which I don't remember. But I do recall that he had parma ham, melon and a Becks beer. I had a pasta dish which burned my mouth and made talking difficult. Our conversation turned largely on opposition politics because at that stage Mr Oppenheimer was still supporting both the UP and the Progressive Party financially. He was troubled by Sir de Villiers Graaff's speech at the most recent conference when the UP adopted the slogan of 'political control over the whole South Africa'. Incidentally, what pleased me was that he and the other two volunteered very early on in our discussion to read my column in the *Sunday Tribune*.

This meeting with Harry Oppenheimer was very important to me because it established the basis of a relationship that lasted until he died in 2000. I found him to be very friendly and to have a genuine interest in the various ventures I asked him to support down the years. He was also responsible for Anglo American funding Anita's research in South Africa.

My meeting with Mr Oppenheimer was on 1 December and I met Prime Minister Verwoerd the next day in his office in the Union Buildings in

Pretoria. The interview was granted on certain conditions. Fanie Olivier, his private secretary, wrote to me as follows: 'The Prime Minister has agreed to see you on the clear understanding that this is not to be a newspaper interview, or for publicity purposes of any kind, but merely an opportunity for you to clarify in your own mind what may be troubling you.' These are his words not mine. Before entering the Prime Minister's office, I asked Olivier how much time I had. 'He will indicate when it's over' was the response.

I have described the meeting with Dr Verwoerd to various people but, given the preconditions, I have never had reason to write it up beyond a few personal notes which I made immediately afterwards. I anticipated having about thirty minutes with him, but instead the conversation – which is something of an exaggeration because he did most of the talking – lasted an hour and a quarter, and when I came out of his office there were about a dozen senior civil servants with files under their arms glaring at me.

To be perfectly frank, I was impressed with him as a person and as somebody who really knew how to get his point of view across. Charming, with a nice sense of humour coupled with a ready smile, clearly highly intelligent and used to getting his way – he was quite confident that his charm and intellect were working on me. But it was a confidence that was devoid of arrogance. We covered a wide range of topics, with him almost inviting my responses. I think he liked the idea of having a discussion with an academic – although he said he no longer had time to read books – it was all official documents and he confirmed the story that he even took them to the toilet. Yes, he needed his afternoon nap and it was true that he changed into his pyjamas.

As regards substantive matters, I put to him the issues I had raised in the correspondence with Dr Muller. Verwoerd would not be drawn on the Rhodesian issue – raging at the time – and didn't introduce anything new on the six meetings he had had with Dag Hammarskjöld, United Nations Secretary-General at the time. My meeting with Dr Verwoerd took place less than a year before his assassination (September 1966) and over the past few years there's been some interesting speculation that Verwoerd was about to make major changes in race relations policy just before he was assassinated. And some of the evidence for this is related to the meetings that he had with Hammarskjöld.

My meeting with John Vorster, Minister of Justice, took place the day after I had seen Dr Verwoerd – and it was quite a contrast. Much later, when I was in Parliament and Vorster was the Prime Minister, we used to play chess together on a Friday or Saturday evening at his Groote Schuur residence. He was a jokey character who enjoyed a laugh and put oodles of apricot jam over our post-chess supper of fried eggs, bacon and sausages. The person I saw that day in his office in Pretoria was rather withdrawn and modest and was very careful not to seem to be intruding in the Prime Minister's domain.

* * *

Politics at UND (as it was called at the time) was accommodated in the Department of History on both the Durban and Pietermaritzburg campuses. Peter Harris, who previously served in the British colonial service, was senior lecturer and ended his academic career as professor of political science in Hong Kong. The department head was shared between Professor Mark Prestwich in Pietermaritzburg and Professor Ken McIntyre in Durban. But the person whom I was closest to and with whom I immediately struck up a strong friendship which has lasted to this day was the historian Andrew Duminy.

The Vice-Chancellor, when I arrived, was the eminent E.G. Malherbe, who had been very close to Jan Smuts and had an enviable reputation as an educationalist. In fact, he was one of the first South Africans to recognise the importance of bilingualism to cognitive development in children and therefore vigorously advocated parallel-medium or dual-medium schools. This was not something favoured at the time by Afrikaans intellectuals. A reason I mention this is that Anita had devoted a lot of her studies at Cornell to the subject as a result of her Canadian and Québec background. And she was to research the topic for her doctorate at Cornell when we moved to Pretoria. She is today an international authority on the subject.

I had little to do with Malherbe but much more with his successor – Owen Horwood. Horwood had been professor of economics at the University of Rhodesia (before it became Zimbabwe) and, of course, was later to be appointed Minister of Finance by Prime Minister Vorster. He then went into politics and became leader of the National Party in Natal.

The subjects I had responsibility for were international relations and political theory at the first- and third-year level. There was no real challenge to this and I had a lot of time to do research and writing. I also had some interesting students whose careers were parallel with mine in later years.

These included Roger Hulley and Renier Schoeman, who had a rather varied political career and is now active in the ANC.

Probably the most publicised event during my two years at UND was the visit to the university of Senator Robert (Bobby) Kennedy, the younger brother of President John F. Kennedy, and his wife Ethel. After keeping the audience waiting for three hours, Kennedy delivered a short punchy speech and followed it up by taking questions from the audience. I hadn't met Robert Kennedy during my stay in the US and had never heard him speak other than on television, and I could see why he had a strong following.

However, I frankly had never come to like him as I thought him overly ambitious, and in his capacity as Attorney General, he all too frequently went beyond the Constitution. But there is no question that on that day in Durban he boosted the campaign against university apartheid. Bobby, sadly, like his brother, was assassinated shortly afterwards.

As with Andrew Duminy, it was at UND that I first met Lawrence Schlemmer, who became one of the country's top sociologists. His office was very close to mine and we got to know each other very well. He made a unique contribution to South African society both academically, through involving distinguished international academics, and from a constitutional point of view. He took Mangosuthu Buthelezi, the Chief Minister of KwaZulu, very seriously and was throughout centrally involved in the Buthelezi Commission and the Indaba, which became very relevant to my career much later when I was Ambassador in London. He was a brilliant, practical (and therefore quite unique) academic and a lovely person, who died rather suddenly in 2011.

10

DIE BEELD AND *RAPPORT* COLUMNS

Not long after settling in Durban I had lunch with Ian Wyllie, who was deputy editor of the *Sunday Tribune* and a very likeable person with an unusually strong interest in international and US politics in particular. In fact, his favourite American personality was Dean Acheson, after whom Anita and I later named our youngest son. In any event, this resulted in me doing a weekly public affairs column which I was told quite quickly acquired a national readership. It came to an end rather suddenly towards the end of the year when I rather foolishly contributed an article in the middle of the week to the daily *Natal Mercury*, which cleverly published it in the same format as the *Tribune* column. The next Sunday I looked in vain for my column.

But unknown to me at the time, I was given another opportunity to write a column when we went to Cape Town for the December vacation. I took the opportunity of meeting with Schalk Pienaar, editor of the Nasionale Pers newspaper *Beeld*, which had recently been established as a Sunday newspaper and would be published in Johannesburg, but Pienaar was still managing it from *Die Burger*'s office in Cape Town. He knew of my *Sunday Tribune* column and I asked him whether he would be interested in my writing for *Beeld*: I would contribute from an English-speaking South African point of view.

By way of background, this was a period of intense ideological rivalry between Afrikaners in the south and Afrikaners in the north. It was reflected in the so-called *verligte–verkrampte* division. All aspects of Afrikaner society, including the National Party, were affected. It expressed itself in the churches and universities (for example, Stellenbosch University was regarded as more liberal than Pretoria) and revolved around issues like the role of the coloured community, petty apartheid, censorship and even literature.

These divisions were reflected in the two big Afrikaans media groups: Nasionale Pers which has of course grown into a global media company, publisher of the daily *Die Burger*; and Afrikaanse Pers with its daily newspaper *Die Transvaler*. The tension between the two was very tangible at that time. While Naspers had a whiff of superiority about it, the only Afrikaans Sunday newspaper, *Dagbreek*, was owned and published by Afrikaanse Pers and it circulated nationally. There were therefore both commercial and political reasons why Nasionale Pers would also want a Sunday paper. Hence the decision to establish *Beeld*, later to be known as *Rapport*, which today is the only Afrikaans Sunday newspaper. At the time I met with Schalk Pienaar the two groups were at each other's throats.

Schalk agreed to my doing a regular column reflecting an English-speaking point of view, and the first column appeared on Sunday, 30 January 1966. However, as this was something of a novelty, the first column had a big Roman numeral I on top of it. Pienaar was shrewdly covering himself if the column bombed. And so it appeared until around the sixth Sunday when the following Monday I received a phone call from Dirk Richard, the editor of *Dagbreek*, which was of course *Beeld*'s competition. He coyly asked me whether I would contribute an article on English-speaking political attitudes for the next Sunday. Of course, I told Schalk of the call when I sent my copy through for that week. That Sunday the Roman figure was missing from my column and I continued to contribute every Sunday for six years. But I don't think Schalk, who became one of my best friends, anticipated the problems I would cause him down the track. I certainly did not expect them. Pienaar knew that he was running a political risk when he took me on. But I don't think even he appreciated just how big a risk it was.

The point has been made that Pienaar was at the centre of the *verligte–verkrampte* struggle. In fact, D.J. Opperman, the famous poet who was also a friend of Pienaar, described him as adopting a broad but incisive political approach when battling *Dagbreek*: 'The battle was against muddled ideas, ridiculous applications of the apartheid regulations, pet ideas regarding the homeland policy, the sore that was Soweto, the destabilising of the National Party which leads to Conservative reactions.' Pienaar's response was to describe *verkramptes* as 'Super Afrikaners', who applied the term 'liberalism' to everybody and everything which deviated from the norm of what had come to be regarded as orthodox – among whom were highly reputed poets like Dirk Opperman, N.P. van Wyk Louw, Breyten Breytenbach and André P Brink.

One last word on the battle between *Beeld* and *Dagbreek* and the Afrikaans Sunday newspaper issue. Joel Mervis, legendary editor of the *Sunday Times*, contributed an analysis of the battle in a trade publication. Mervis concluded: 'It would not be easy to challenge the assertion that *Die Beeld* is easily the most spectacular enterprise in the history of South African newspapers. I can certainly think of nothing to equal its astonishing growth … The "Beeld Spectacular", as one might describe its story, would not amount to much were it not for its remarkable editor, Mr Schalk Pienaar.'

Pienaar acknowledged that there was an increasing hostility to me in Afrikaans politics – although he knew the content and essence and semi-intellectual tone of my contributions had remained the same. But he went on to explain that people and institutions that wanted to get at Prime Minister Vorster but did not have the guts to do so directly, chose to go for him by attacking the newspaper and, said Pienaar, Denis Worrall in particular. This was particularly the case in the Transvaal. In fact, at one of the National Party's provincial annual conferences, a number of delegates threatened to withhold their support unless the party repudiated Denis Worrall. And at an NP Cape conference, P.W. Botha got a mutual friend to ask Schalk Pienaar whether continuing to publish Denis Worrall was worth the trouble.

So it was that Pienaar felt obliged in September 1968 to contribute an editorial personally justifying the column. 'If an Afrikaner wants to know – and he should want to know – how an enlightened English-speaking South African sees a particular situation, it should be possible for him to read this in *Beeld*.' He added that his editorial colleagues favoured retaining the column and circulation figures supported that view.

But the best was still to come. As a result of pressure from the Prime Minister, in February 1969 Pienaar wrote to Hubert Coetzee, managing director of Nasionale Pers, enquiring whether the group had an official view in relation to the question of publishing André Brink and myself. To be specific Pienaar wrote: 'While there are differences of opinion regarding these two, my opinion is that both these columns are highly valuable to *Beeld*. Brink is without a doubt the most brilliant writer in Afrikaans and Worrall is very widely read, also by people who don't agree with him.' Shortly after writing this letter he received a personal response from Hubert Coetzee, which was: 'Schalk, ek vra jou: wie die donner is redakteur van *Beeld*? Jy of John Vorster?' (Who the hell is editor of *Beeld*? You or John Vorster?) It is a quote which has become a classic statement of editorial independence.

The column enriched my understanding of South African politics. After all, from 1948 most major developments in the country were very largely determined by Afrikaners and their response to the general South African situation. In fact, the response of Afrikaners to the big challenges the country faced would very largely determine whether the transition from apartheid to a more inclusive society would be a relatively peaceful one. That was the assumption underlying my initial entry to politics and, later, to my resignation of the ambassadorship in London and the decision to contest the Helderberg constituency in 1987.

11

NEW NATION

I have mentioned before how, during my stay in the US, I very much enjoyed the numerous intellectual periodicals that were available. I am referring to publications like *National Review*, *Commentary*, *The New Republic* and *The Nation*. I missed them very much on my return to South Africa and decided I would try to establish something similar as there wasn't anything like them.

I shared the idea with Anita and some confidants and we agreed on *New Nation* as the name. I accordingly registered New Nation Publications (Pty) Ltd as a necessary preliminary to all the other registrations that were required. As regards finances, none of us had much money and the main cost of printing I covered on a monthly basis through advertising and subscriptions, which Anita took care of. As regards advertising, which was my responsibility, we aimed to get four full-page ads per issue, and achieved this after three or four issues. Certain corporate executives liked our message and guaranteed an ad almost on a per issue basis. These included Naas Steenkamp of General Mining, Harry Oppenheimer of Anglo, Anton Rupert of Rembrandt, Dr Conrad Strauss of Standard Bank, Tom Boardman of Nedbank, Dr Frans Cronje of SA Breweries, and Dr Albert Wessels of Toyota.

I described the goal of *New Nation* in the maiden editorial in the first edition which appeared in August 1967. 'It will be a forum of opinion and commentary spanning the entire intellectual spectrum. Its pages will be open to all opinions without prejudice or favour. Everyone connected with the venture would like to see it grow into a highly sophisticated, tasteful and intellectually stimulating publication, which will not only be a credit to thinking South Africans, but will reflect a truly contemporary image of our country to readers abroad.' This was the concept shared by those who formed with me the first editorial board – Simon Brand, Andrew Duminy, John Dugard, Adam Kolczynski, Peter Titlestad, Malvern van Wyk Smith and Kit Hoffmann, who had journalistic experience and would help with the practical aspect of getting it out. Although she was not on the editorial board initially, Anita was to play a major role in *New Nation*'s management.

Over time the editorial board was restructured to include associate editors and assistant editors for specific topics. So Barry Ronge and John van Zyl became assistant editors for films; Robin Lee for education; Hannes Meiring for art; Mario Schiess and Pieter Scholtz for theatre; Deon Fourie for military affairs; Anita Worrall for behaviour; Bill Yeowart and Adolph Lichtigfeld for books. And the board was strengthened by the addition of Johan Degenaar, Adam Small, H.W. van der Merwe, John Chettle and W.A. (Bill) de Klerk. We received approaches quite early on to carry articles in Afrikaans but, much as we would have liked to, we were conscious that our international readership was growing. In any event, a very high proportion of our contributions came from Afrikaners and we did publish Afrikaans poetry.

To many readers these names may have little meaning but others will understand what my pioneering editors and I achieved. We brought together the most extraordinary collection of relevant thinking people in South Africa at that time. That they were all with one exception white South Africans was a reflection of the time. We encouraged youthful readers with essay competitions and the winner of one such competition was a young boy called Dennis Davis, now a judge. As regards the marketing of *New Nation*, nobody could have helped us more than Hennie Serfontein of the *Sunday Times*. We ensured that he had a copy as it appeared and was alerted to what we thought was of national interest in every issue. Hennie made sure it was carried in the next edition of South Africa's widest circulating newspaper.

Andrew Duminy, in his recently published book *The Past Is Present*, has written this elegant appreciation of *New Nation*. 'I became involved in the launching of the monthly journal *New Nation*, the first issue of which appeared in August 1967. The moving spirit behind it was Denis Worrall.... I was overseas at the time but enthusiastically supported the idea because it seemed to me that so little free and challenging debate was taking place in South Africa.

'Although none of us had any experience in journalism or in commerce, *New Nation* was a surprising success and ran for nearly eight years. This was due almost entirely to Denis's great enthusiasm, together with his ability to identify topics of interest and solicit articles from a very wide range of people. Among the contributors were Nadine Gordimer, Adam Small, Heribert Adam, Lawrie Schlemmer, Barry Ronge, Roy MacNab, Tim Couzens, Guy Butler, Wimpie de Klerk, Colin Eglin, W.A. (Bill) de Klerk, Pierre Hugo, Japie Basson and Marais Steyn. Among those who published their poetry were Mike Kirkwood, Christopher Hope and Jeremy Cronin. A regular contributor was Gus Ferguson, a young Cape Town pharmacist, who provided many whimsical drawings under the nom-de-plume "Nosugref". He subsequently made a name for himself as a poet and cartoonist.'

My editorship of *New Nation* began in August 1967 with the first issue. It ended in the March 1974 edition with an announcement under the heading 'New Editor':

The need for a publication which would be open to all points of view and which would be seen to be intellectually and politically independent was an important reason I established *New Nation* seven years ago. Among the distinguished intellectuals on its masthead are several persons with known political views and affiliations which they have not hesitated to promote, and as editor it has been my task to ensure a balance between the points of view represented. However, as a consequence of my decision to speak in favour of the National Party in the present general election campaign, I'm withdrawing from the editorial board so as to avoid any suggestion of compromising the independence all of us – readers, contributors, advertisers, and editors – so much appreciate about *New Nation*. Professor André de Villiers, director of the Institute for the Study of English in Africa at Rhodes University, has assumed the editorship until further notice.

André edited the July 1974 issue from Grahamstown but afterwards there was a gap in publication. *New Nation* was then taken over by a corporate executive in Johannesburg. The October, November, December 1974 issues appeared, although with the same editorial board but no indication of who the editor was, and a changed format, but the December number proved to be the last.

12

My Move to Unisa

Before I went to America I was a member of the South African Institute of International Affairs, a highly reputed organisation with strong academic connections and solid support from the private sector. At UND I reconnected with the organisation. The director was John Barratt, whom I first met when he was Director of Information in the South African UN Embassy in New York. The Institute had an endowed chair of international relations commemorating General Smuts' role in world affairs, whose incumbent then was Professor Ben Cockram.

These activities brought me into touch with Professor M.H.H. (Mike) Louw, who was Professor of International Relations and head of the Department of Politics at the University of South Africa in Pretoria – the biggest department in the country. Professor Louw was a unique South African. He was an Afrikaner who had completed his primary and initial graduate studies at the University of Pretoria before getting a scholarship to the University of Chicago. He obtained a doctorate and joined the United Nations as a technical and administrative adviser based first in New York but for most of his working life in South America. He spoke perfect Portuguese and Spanish and was married to Hannah, a delightful and spirited Brazilian of Czech origin. On retirement from the UN, he returned to South Africa and headed up the Department of Political Science at Unisa.

We met at various SAIIA functions, and to this day I clearly remember the impact he made on me. He was highly sophisticated, experienced in the ways of the world with a knowledge of world affairs that was impressive, and yet he remained basically an Afrikaner. He also was a person with a unique openness to ideas. And therefore when in August 1966 he told me he needed a senior lecturer in political science and asked me whether I would be interested, there was no question in my mind that, aside from the promotion, this was a person I would like to work with. However, initially there were some important matters that needed to be sorted out.

While at UND, as a member of the Department of Psychology, Anita continued with research for her Cornell doctorate and enjoyed the lecturing and collegiality. But it was not clear what the situation would be in Pretoria if we moved there. And of course there were also people in Durban who told her that, given Pretoria's predominant Afrikaans character, as an immigrant she would find it difficult to settle there. There was also the question of whether she would be able to continue with her research. These issues fell away when they were really tested. But an important factor in influencing the situation was Professor Louw and his wife, Hannah, who charmed Anita. As far as the research aspect was concerned, it turned out that Pretoria would be a more suitable site for the field research which Anita needed to undertake.

I took up the appointment as senior lecturer in political science at Unisa in January 1967. Anita and I exchanged an apartment in Berea, Durban, for one in Sunnyside, Pretoria, and a very different way of life. Contrary to all expectations, it was a much more exciting and stimulating life. Unisa is the biggest distance-learning institution in the world. It formed a model for the better-known Open University in the United Kingdom. Today it uses all forms of digital communication, but when I joined at the beginning of 1967 course notes or lectures were written up and printed in book form and lecturer–student communication was largely by correspondence. I was fortunate in joining a department which was well established with several well-known lecturers. These included Ben Roux in public administration, Willem Kleynhans in South African politics, Deon Fourie in international relations and, of course, Professor Mike Louw. To be perfectly frank, it was not the most challenging of situations or the most demanding in terms of time, and I was able to begin thinking of producing a book.

Pretoria at that time was a very interesting place to be, as Afrikanerdom was cooking. In 1966 Professor Willem de Klerk of the Department of Philosophy in Potchefstroom University, and brother of F.W. de Klerk, delivered a speech which had far-reaching consequences. He distinguished between Afrikaners whom he described as *verligtes*, who were people open to change and were therefore reform-minded, and Afrikaners whom he described as *verkramptes*, who were opposed to change in general and to change in existing patterns of race relations in particular.

There was nothing particularly profound about this speech, but the timing set in motion a process of polarisation which climaxed three years later when Dr Albert Hertzog, a Cabinet minister, broke away from the National Party and established the Herstigte (Reconstituted) Nasionale Party. Pretoria was the centre of the *verligte–verkrampte* struggle or, as Afrikaners put it, *Broedertwis*. Ironically, a major player in this conflict was an English-speaker named S.E.D. Brown, who produced a right-wing monthly publication called *SA Observer*. And as Brown put it in one issue, somewhat reminiscent of President Trump: 'The Observer speaks not for the big businessman or the industrialist or the new-rich, nor is he a person who hob-nobs with the mighty. He is the little man, whether he be an Afrikaans teacher, worker, clergyman, farmer or professional man, and he is and will always remain the backbone of the White nation.'

I naturally took an intense interest in what was happening and found myself quite regularly devoting my column on Sundays in the *Beeld* to the issues involved, which frequently resulted in my being pilloried by *Hoofstad*, the *verkrampte*-supporting newspaper in Pretoria. This in itself was not a bad thing, because it resulted in Anita and me being sought after by Embassy people wanting to know more.

But what was very pleasing was that from very early on in our stay in Pretoria we attracted a lot of young *verligtes* – writers, poets, artists and young professionals. They included the poet Phil du Plessis, the theologian Brian Johanson, the philosopher Leon Coetzee, Ridley Beeton, the head of English at Unisa, and Pierre Hugo, an Africanist. Lending gravity was a person like Judge Victor Hiemstra; adding fun was the painter Walter Battiss; and offering inside perspectives were Tertius Myburgh, then editor of the *Pretoria News*, and Pik Botha, member of Parliament in Pretoria and his wife, Helena. Lifelong friends whom we met very early on in Pretoria were John and Lola Newbury. Regular visitors from Johannesburg included Otto Krause, Jonathan Suzman, Bill Yeowart, and John and Judith Chettle. Our modest apartment became an intellectual salon to which Anita's cosmopolitanism added enormously. But I believe Anita and I both learnt that people didn't come to our table to eat. They came for the discussion, the exchange of opinions, the joy and the laughter and – don't forget it – the *skinner*!

For both Anita and me, the four years in Pretoria were creative and productive. Anita was able to complete her research well within expectations and present the results to be awarded her PhD by Cornell in 1972. Even today her work is regularly cited internationally.

Although my book *South Africa: Government and Politics* was published in 1971, when I had already transferred to Wits, the work on it was done at Unisa. It was intended to fill the long-felt need in political science circles for an introductory textbook and general guide to the institutions of government and the processes of politics in this country. This is what inspired me as the innovator and overall editor and, I believe, my co-contributors. I think we acknowledged that the need itself reflected the fact that political science had arrived as an academic discipline in South African universities. John Barratt of the Institute of International Affairs; Peter Harris, my colleague from UND; Gerrit Olivier from Rand Afrikaans University; and Ben Roux from Unisa all made splendid contributions, with Professor Marcus Arkin from Rhodes University presenting a solid overview of the South African economy. The publishers, Van Schaik of Pretoria, shared our enthusiasm all the way. In fact, the senior brother Jan van Schaik treated it as his baby. His love of books and producing books was extraordinary.

13

APPOINTMENT TO WITS

When Ben Cockram, who held the Smuts chair of International Relations at Wits, retired, Professor Mike Louw was appointed to succeed him in April 1970. The Department of International Relations was, and is, accommodated in Jan Smuts House, the home of the Institute of International Affairs. The director of the institute, and therefore the person responsible for the administration of the building, was John Barratt, a delightful and able person whom I first met in New York when he was with South Africa's UN mission. Toward the end of 1970 Louw encouraged me to apply for the senior lecturer position, which I did, and I was appointed in February 1971.

A number of reasons prompted my interest in an appointment to Wits. Firstly, I wanted to get back to lecturing and dealing with real students. And when I did, I found Wits students stimulating and interested. Another was the fact that the Department of International Relations at Wits, given its close connection to the Institute and Jan Smuts House with its steady stream of international researchers, was the centre point of international studies in South Africa at that time. Also of attraction was the library. This was the library Jan Smuts had built up on his farm outside Pretoria. It included the most magnificent and varied collection of books reflecting his intellectual virtuosity and depth. Many of the books were signed first editions of books by famous scholars and scientists around the world. The library, or a relic of it, had been built into Jan Smuts House on the Wits campus.

Anita's situation was also an important factor in wanting to make the move from Pretoria to Johannesburg. Quite early on after our arrival in Pretoria she had applied for a post at Unisa but had been declined. Fortunately, she had her research work to do and also at about that time she met Joyce Fein in Johannesburg who had established Crossroads, a school for children with learning difficulties. And Joyce, on hearing of Anita's availability, immediately offered her a post as a psychologist. This meant that until we made the move Anita travelled by car between Pretoria and Johannesburg a couple of days a week.

As I have indicated, we already had lots of friends in Johannesburg and the move represented something like a consolidation of us as a family entity. We bought a house in the suburb of Linden, not a particularly grand house but a solid house with a very large garden and a fruit orchard. Japie Basson, one of my favourite politicians whose constituency was in Johannesburg but whose home was in Cape Town, used to spend the better part of Sundays with us in that garden as he was a great believer in the regenerative power of sunshine.

When we moved to Johannesburg we had been married for six years and we both wanted to start a family, something we knew was not as easily done as said. But in May 1971 Anita fell pregnant only to lose the child at six months. It was naturally an enormous disappointment, given that the pregnancy had not come easily. On professional advice we chose to adopt a baby boy of seven months, whom we named Christian John, after my father and me. To our delight Lyndon Matthew was born on 10 January 1974 and Elliot Dean on 10 September 1975, almost as though Chris's presence had eased the process. Anita continued to be associated with Crossroads, and did some lecturing at Rand Afrikaans University, but this was more in the way of keeping abreast of developments rather than as an active career, and in line with her belief that even professional women need to give priority to their children at an early age. In the meantime Anita's mother, who was widowed in Montréal, had come out to South Africa, where she remarried shortly afterwards.

Our social and professional life in Johannesburg was no less active than in Pretoria. We got to know Alec and Sarah Pienaar, who at one stage had been at the University of Cape Town with me, and the Newburys moved to Johannesburg as John's career in the motor business blossomed. We reconnected with my old university mate Norman Lowenthal and his wife Pam, one of Johannesburg's most gracious couples. A visit to his subterranean private wine cellar was an unforgettable experience and their Friday night dinners drew the crème de la crème of the Johannesburg Jewish community.

There is a natural consanguinity between political scientists and politicians on the one hand and journalists on the other. In my case this was particularly strong as over time I aspired to be both. I developed relations with most editors at the time. I had an excellent relationship with Joel Mervis of the *Sunday Times* and Johnny Johnson of the rival *Sunday Express*. In fact, Mervis offered me a column but quite correctly said he suspected Schalk Pienaar would not agree to my writing for the *Sunday Times*, given my *Beeld* column. He was of course absolutely right in that respect and we never pursued it.

The rivalry between Joel Mervis and Johnny Johnson was so intense that it divided the Jewish community of Johannesburg. Johnson was known to be a very difficult man, so much so that the only person who could work with him was his wife, which introduced a certain intimacy to meetings with him. John Scott, once editor of the *Cape Times*, tells the story of the young journalist who, after working long and hard on a piece, took it to Johnson, who looked over the flimsy and said: 'You want my opinion of this?' And promptly put it in his mouth, chewed it and spat it into the wastepaper basket. I also got to know Tertius Myburgh when he was editor of *Pretoria News* and subsequently editor of the *Sunday Times*. I don't, by the way, accept the charge levelled against him after his death that he was a spy for the government.

I had established media contacts in Cape Town who, within a couple of years, would be playing an important role in my career. Tony Heard, editor of the *Cape Times*, and John Scott by that time were very good friends, as were Alf Ries and Ebbe Dommisse, who would of course soon step into the big shoes of Piet Cilliers. But a surprising relationship was with Laurence Gandar of the *Rand Daily Mail*. While we had our differences, in June 1966 after I had complimented him on a supplement which the *Mail* had produced, he wrote by way of a reply: 'I greatly appreciate what you had to say about the supplement. May I, in turn, record that I always read your articles in *Die Beeld*, and although your approach on national affairs is somewhat different from mine, I think that what you have to say is always worthwhile and, if I may add, said very well. Perhaps one day you will write something for the *Rand Daily Mail*.' And I also got to know John Patten, editor of *The Star* and the father of a couple of distinguished journalists of my generation.

From an academic point of view Rand Afrikaans University, which was very new, was a major source of connections under the vice-chancellorship of Pieter de Lange. But, to be perfectly frank, I expanded and developed the relations I already had with Potchefstroom. What is already clear is that Potchefstroom through Willem de Klerk's 1966 speech and sequel, and through the journal *Woord en Daad*, was at the heart of the developments within Afrikanerdom. The person at Potchefstroom whom I became very fond of and who figured in this was Professor Hennie Coetzee, who was originally trained as an anthropologist. He was a modest person and quite shy. He had to be drawn out, and with John Barratt's help, we increasingly engaged him and several colleagues in the Institute of International Affairs' activities. He typically would begin to speak on a major topic by saying, 'Look, I am just a simple *boertjie* from Potchefstroom' and end by wowing the audience.

Professor Coetzee attended several dinner parties at our home in Linden. I remember one of them in particular where among the other guests were Zach de Beer, Madeleine van Biljon, Otto Krause and Schalk Pienaar, editor of *Rapport* for which I still wrote the column. M.T. Moerane was a regular as was Rykie van Reenen, of whom Schalk used to tell the following story. He noticed from her chequebook that she banked with Standard Bank and not, as was more general among Afrikaners, with Volkskas. Her explanation was that when she was a student, only Standard Bank would give her an overdraft to buy a motorcycle!

As I look back, 1971 was a very active year for me both from an academic point of view and in terms of public engagement. I added quite considerably to my academic publications list and through my journalism. In a report published in the *Sunday Times*, Julian Kraft quoted an editorial I contributed to *New Nation* to the effect that 'In the next five years democracy will come under tremendous pressure in South Africa and the government will be tempted to rely increasingly on executive action and the bypassing of the legislature'. I am quoted as saying that 'The threat to democratic values and procedures would arise not so much from the policies of any particular political party, but from the circumstances which are likely to develop'.

One thing I must stress is that, while many academic colleagues disagreed with me and disagreed strongly with me, at no time did I experience any official university disapproval of my public pronouncements or of my journalism. This was notwithstanding my criticism from very early on in my academic career of the English-speaking intelligentsia and its commitment to a 'common society' concept of liberalism. My starting point in this regard was Alfred Hoernlé, whom a latter-day American scholar describes as the most authoritative analyst of liberalism in South Africa. On this basis I completely concur with the distinguished University of Natal professor of law, Anthony Mathews, when he said the fundamental weakness of liberal thinking had been its 'basic aversion to pluralism and a deeply ingrained suspicion of the group as a political category'.

This version of liberalism ignored the reality of the modern state, which holds that individual freedom is mediated through groups and institutional associations. This is an issue which is highly relevant to the future of democracy in this country.

14

RHODES UNIVERSITY AND GRAHAMSTOWN

In late 1972 I was offered the position of head of the Department of Political Science at the University of Rhodesia in what was then Salisbury. The terms that were offered to me were generous and accommodating. So I at first accepted the position but, to be frank, not whole-heartedly. I knew that Anita was against going to Rhodesia, and personally I wondered about the wisdom of leaving the South African academic system and also giving up my role as a commentator on the South African political situation. Also, any political ambitions I might develop, which I believed would be enriched by a period of living elsewhere in southern Africa, would nonetheless be realised in the Republic. And what I did not understand at the time of accepting the Rhodesian offer was that there were other acceptable opportunities for advancement in South Africa itself.

One was heading up the Institute of Social and Economic Research at Rhodes University in Grahamstown. Marcus Arkin, who was Professor of Economics at Rhodes, obviously knew that Hobart Houghton, then Director of the Institute, was due to retire and strongly supported me as a potential successor. Once he learnt that I was tempted to go to Salisbury – it was reported in several newspapers – he intervened directly by explaining the situation to the Rhodes Vice-Chancellor, Professor J.M. Hyslop, and gaining his tacit support for my candidacy. The result was that shortly afterwards I was invited to visit Grahamstown to acquaint myself with the directorship and what it entailed and meet with the appointment board. This included, among others, Professor Hyslop, Guy Butler, and the legendary Winnie Maxwell, the historian reputed to having taught more professors of history than anybody else. Central to my presentation was the history and political role of English-speaking South Africans, something which Professor Maxwell liked very much. It also tied in with Grahamstown as the focal point of the 1820 Settlers Monument and the activities around it. As a consequence I was offered the appointment from 1 July 1973.

There is something attractive about university towns. Ithaca in New York was one such. Central to employment was education – Cornell University and Ithaca College. If there were any very rich people, nobody knew of them or where they lived. Accordingly, the economy of Ithaca – its retail outlets, its restaurants and its entertainment centres – were focused at a middle class at a sophisticated level.

Grahamstown is a university town and more. The main source of employment, as was the case in Ithaca, is education. There are about twelve well-established and nationally recognised public and private schools in Grahamstown in addition to the university. Grahamstown is also rich in the activities one associates with an educational centre – art galleries, museums, theatres and research institutions in different areas. And there was a further reason for Grahamstown's importance. It was the seat of the Eastern Cape division of the Supreme Court of South Africa. Therefore, among its residents were judges, advocates and a good number of law firms.

But the dominant ethos of Grahamstown springs from the fact that it was the centre point of the 1820 Settler movement to South Africa. This is reflected in the architecture and the values attached to this feature. Anita and I found when we first arrived in Grahamstown that this was a very important theme of interest and conversation. We managed to sell our house in Linden quite quickly and were interested in finding something appropriate in Grahamstown. We were expected to be interested in acquiring an 1820 Settler cottage or house. Malvern van Wyk Smith of the English Department, and an old friend, had just bought one, and his pride and pleasure was very evident. He was following in the steps of Guy Butler, whose beautiful old house was right next to the main entrance to the university. But we bought, a touch extravagantly, the former official residence of the Vice-Chancellor. It was a modern house with a swimming pool and overlooked most of the university's playing fields.

Our reception within the university could not have been warmer – even the Vice-Chancellor wrote us a welcoming note – and Marcus Arkin was there to introduce me to appropriate faculty members. The very competent

René Vroom, who became my secretary, organised an introduction and welcome to the resident fellows in the centre at that time. These included Norman Bromberger, Jeffrey Butler, Jeff Opland, and Philip and Iona Mayer.

My task as director was essentially to ensure that research fellows got the support that they needed; that research funding which was made available for particular projects was appropriately allocated; and generally market the Institute both nationally and internationally. In this respect I set up a reading room in the centre which drew newspapers from all over the country (this was long before the digital era), something which was greatly appreciated by foreign students, and I persuaded South African Associated Newspapers, through Tertius Myburgh, to make an annual research grant specifically for political research. While this was all quite demanding, I found the time to get on with my own research and writing programme. The work I did at that time on the political contribution of English-speakers to South African politics was well received. The paper I delivered to the 'English-Speaking South Africa Today' conference in July 1974 set out my personal approach and views.

One aspect of research which I felt had been neglected was the media. Incidentally, a quaint and delightful feature of Grahamstown is *Grocott's Mail*, the oldest independent newspaper in South Africa. It is now very sensibly owned by the Rhodes School of Journalism. I, of course, continued to edit *New Nation* (it was printed in Port Elizabeth) and write my weekly column for *Rapport*. My founding and dominant role in *New Nation* for more than seven years and the column were the reason the Jaycees in 1973 awarded me one of their 'Outstanding Young South African' awards for what they described as my 'bridge-building role.'

So for me personally Rhodes was a stimulating and generally happy experience, but it was less so for Anita. She found herself excluded from the main thrust of the Grahamstown community. She had been offered a lectureship in psychology but declined it on account of Chris, who at that stage was nine months old. And in 1973 she fell pregnant with Lyndon, who was born in Port Elizabeth on 10 January 1974. So she had quite a handful to deal with.

It was against that background, and the probability of a general election being called in 1974, that I began to think in terms of taking the political plunge.

15

ENTRY TO POLITICS:
A GRAND ENTRANCE

The decision to leave the relative comfort and security of academia for the hustle and bustle and insecurities of politics is obviously not something one does without very serious thought. Aside from what personal role I would play and what contribution I would make, there clearly were considerations which went way beyond my personal interest and satisfaction. I was happily married to a loving and clever woman with a lovely son and another child on the way. While I had the advantage of being relatively young and healthy, I had minimal financial reserves. And once I had made a political commitment, I wouldn't have been able to return to academic life as a political scientist. I used to tell my students that it was essential if you went into politics that you should have established yourself in some other career first so that you had a fallback position – because politics is not a job or a career, it is a vocation, in Afrikaans a *roeping*. I was fortunate in having a potential fallback position in that I had advanced legal qualifications and, as I will explain, I didn't waste any time in turning them into a reality.

South African political folklore was full of stories of how you wangled your way into a constituency. Unbeknown to everybody, you made a careful study of selected constituencies. Ideally, the sitting member of Parliament should be old and ready to croak. Ideally, he (or she) should be the biggest attorney in town or one of the richest farmers in the district. In both instances it would help you greatly if they both had ugly unmarried daughters who would find your attentions irresistible.

However, to be serious, the hard way of getting a constituency in the old South Africa was more like this. You selected your constituency as in the way described, went into local government and became mayor, got yourself elected to the Provincial Council, and after that, with just patience and keeping your nose clean, the succession was yours. But in all instances you needed to be a member of a political party and have done your party's service.

Of course, none of this was open to me. I couldn't even claim the backing of a political party as I was not a member of a party. In terms of the Act of Union, which was the constitution of South Africa, the Senate, or upper house of Parliament, included eight members (or two from each province) appointed by the President on the recommendation of the Prime Minister. And in terms of the constitution the President, in appointing at least four of these persons, 'was to be guided mainly by their thorough acquaintance, by reason of their official experience, or otherwise, with the reasonable wishes and wants of the coloured races in South Africa'. The challenge to me was clear. I had to persuade Prime Minister John Vorster to recommend me to the State President for appointment as one of these four Senators – a challenge, indeed, bearing in mind the irritation my *Beeld* column, and presumably my other expressions of opinion, had caused him.

I had previously met Vorster when he was Minister of Justice and I was at the University of Natal. I didn't have any difficulty in setting up an appointment with him, which took place in his office in Cape Town on 23 November 1973. The date of the general election had not yet been announced and I would therefore describe the discussion as exploratory. He knew I was not a member of the National Party and therefore hardly likely to qualify for a constituency. So the discussion quite naturally turned to the Senate. If an appointment were a possibility, what province would I prefer? I said the Cape, where I had grown up. Vorster said it would be easier if it were the Transvaal but he had a problem with the Cape. He said I needed to get the Cape leader, P.W. Botha, behind me. I agreed to follow up by meeting Botha.

I met with P.W. Botha in Cape Town on 13 December 1973 and explained my situation to him exactly as I had to the Prime Minister. Although he was similarly welcoming, there were no commitments on his part. I agreed to meet again with him in February. He asked me whether I would make a couple of speeches on behalf of some of the NP candidates when the election was called, which I accepted to do. I followed this up with a letter to Prime Minister Vorster, telling him of the meeting with the Cape leader and informing him of our agreement to meet again in February.

Incidentally, it did concern me that, once the general election was called and I appeared on platforms, this might have repercussions at the university; but it did not. In the first place I had cleared it with Vice-Chancellor Hyslop and, secondly, because Malvern van Wyk Smith of the English Department was the Progressive Federal Party (PFP) candidate in the Albany constituency. Also the speeches I made were extremely '*verlig*' in content and tone.

The election took place on 24 April 1974 and there was no question that the government would reconstitute the Senate. Obviously, this wasn't going to happen immediately and patience was advised. But one began to read of appointments which were being made, yet I heard nothing.

Over the weekend of 18 May we planned to visit our friends the Newburys in East London. That Saturday morning, before leaving Grahamstown, I phoned P.W. Botha. He told me that what I was asking him to do was very difficult: I had no record in the party, etc. He was clearly negative. I told him that was not my impression of the Prime Minister's position, and I got Botha to promise to speak to the Prime Minister. I gave him the Newburys' number in East London. When we got to East London, the first thing our host told me was that P.W. Botha had called. It was around lunch-time but nevertheless I phoned him. Yes, he had spoken to the Prime Minister. It was a very difficult call to make because the Prime Minister was on his son's farm and it was a party line. But the Prime Minister wanted me. However, I should understand this made his (Botha's) position very difficult because he would have to sack people. But the Prime Minister said he wanted me and that was that. Our lunch was a celebratory one!

The following week the Prime Minister called me twice requesting personal details. And on 29 May (my 39th birthday) Vorster told me the announcement of my appointment would be made on the evening of 30 May and would be applicable from that date. I immediately wrote to Professor Hyslop: 'As I informed you late yesterday afternoon, the Prime Minister has asked me to make myself available for a recommendation to the State President for appointment to the Senate to fill one of the two such appointments for the Cape Province. This is an honour and an opportunity which is very difficult for me to pass up and I have accordingly advised the Prime Minister that I would be pleased to accept.' I wrote to the Prime Minister and the Cape leader, P.W. Botha, on the same day (5 June), thanking them for having made this entry to public life possible.

What amazed me was the public reaction to the appointment.

Congratulations and good wishes from Cabinet ministers and government members of Parliament I expected. But among the hundreds of best wishes I received there were those who combined both congratulations on the appointment to the post and, given my record, the hope that I would achieve something with it. These included people like Professor Newell Stultz of Brown University, Ton Vosloo, Japie Basson, John Dugard, Ellen Hellmann, Gerrit Olivier, Pierre Hugo, Bill Yeowart, Guy Butler ('You know my views and you will not be surprised if I express the hope that you will continue to be *verlig*, in fact as *verlig* as any government person can be!'), Simon Brand, Norman Lowenthal, Glenn Babb and Barend van Niekerk. Hobart Houghton, my predecessor in the Institute at Rhodes, was the first person to wish me well, and one of the more 'official' communications came from retired Senator Paul Sauer: 'My congratulations on your appointment to the Senate. Although I think it is a rather dull place, I hope you will enjoy it and I'm sure that you will be an asset to it.'

We sold our house in Grahamstown and bought one in Oranjezicht, which is on the slopes of Table Mountain above Cape Town. The house was on Molteno Road, quite high up on the mountain with a sweeping view across the Peninsula. It offered easy and quick access to Parliament. Anita, who now had three young boys to take care of, would in the course of time establish her practice in the same area.

16

THE SENATE: MY FIRST EXPERIENCE OF PARLIAMENT

The chairman of the Senate was Jan de Klerk, father of F.W. de Klerk, the future President. I think Senator De Klerk took a liking to me and was tolerant of the gaffes I made in the beginning. By contrast, as was to be expected, the opposition went for me with all guns blazing. An exception was Bill Horak, the leader of the opposition in the Senate. He was later to become one of the more constructive members of the Constitutional Committee (of which I was chairperson) of the President's Council. He had an excellent understanding of the parliamentary system and of parliamentary procedures and had a genuine intellectual interest in politics.

As regards the government members, they were relaxed in their positions. Most of them were over 60 and weren't interested in further advancement. In fact, I was almost overwhelmed by unpublicised requests conveyed to me in the cloakroom or over a cup of coffee to substitute for them on this or that piece of legislation.

As the youngest member of the Senate there was an understanding of my ambition. So, for example, while most Senators shared offices in Marks Building, I had an office to myself which was available to me year round, given that we lived in Cape Town. It was there that I completed the last few subjects for my LLB, started at UCT but completed through Unisa. And it was there that I prepared myself for admission to the Cape Bar.

As a member of the National Party caucus and having declared my interest in foreign affairs and all aspects of race relations, I joined those committees and spoke in those debates. And looking through the Hansard reports and press reports of that time, I made some pretty advanced public pronouncements obviously of a highly *verligte* nature (in the political idiom of the time), which I could do because I was an appointed Senator and, secondly, because everybody knew that I only became a member of the National Party after my appointment as a Senator. I devoted my maiden speech to promoting the interests of the coloured community. I opposed censorship and book bannings. I made the case for English-speakers to play a mediating role in South Africa. I backed and praised Brian Bamford for a speech calling for the government to let races mix freely. Of this the *Cape Times* wrote: 'Senator Denis Worrall comes out to the embarrassment of his Nationalist colleagues, to back Brian Bamford and praised him for being constructive.'

I positioned myself very clearly on the left wing of the National Party with a highly critical speech of Dr Andries Treurnicht, the powerful right-winger who in time came to head the breakaway Conservative Party. And in a debate at the University of Cape Town, reported by the *Cape Times* under the heading 'Worrall urges government to move more boldly', I said I was committed to the creation of a political system in which citizenship would be realised for all South Africans. Shortly afterwards, in what was supposed to be a closed meeting of Stellenbosch academics, I was reported under the headlines 'Proposals will bring full citizenship – Senator Worrall'. This was a reference to certain proposals which the Cabinet had approved and to which I had contributed.

Steve Biko's death and the manner of his dying (in police detention) troubled me very deeply, as I have no doubt it did the great majority of South Africans. But there were some people, even in high office (and I refer to Minister Jimmy Kruger), who responded callously to what was a disgrace and an enormous tragedy. In a public statement which was carried by several newspapers, I not only expressed deep regret but went on to say, 'I am not speaking out of compassion or sympathy alone but also because the future of all of us depends on whether we can come to grips with each other and work out a *modus vivendi*. For we, each of us, have sufficient power to make life impossible for the other.'

I also adopted a strong liberal position relating to private schools and their freedom to choose their pupils. Under the heading 'Let schools decide – Worrall', *The Star* reported: 'As Transvaal school inspectors were due to begin quizzing principals of multi-racial church schools today as a first step to closing them down unless black pupils were expelled, Senator Denis Worrall stated that private schools should be allowed to decide for themselves whom they would admit. Worrall said that attendance of private schools was voluntary and the Roman Catholic decision to open the schools was presumably taken with the approval of the parents involved.'

My role in the Senate offered me, particularly as one of the appointed Senators, the opportunity of developing a political persona I needed to carry over into politics – the values, concepts and principles which I had developed in my academic career and which formed the substance of my contribution to *New Nation* and to my political columns. I think within a year of being in the Senate most people knew where I stood on major issues and how I would respond to challenges as they arose.

* * *

Within eighteen months of my appointment to the Senate, a by-election came up in the Durban North constituency. This seat had been won by the United Party at successive elections but, given the divisions within the UP, the PFP were expected to put up a good fight. In Harry Pitman the PFP had an adventurous and imaginative candidate (something of an athlete, he believed in racing local trains over measured distances) with an attractive and lively wife who led his campaign.

I don't know who first suggested I should stand but the announcement was made by the Prime Minister and made rather dramatically at the end of a speech in the House. I accepted the offer of the candidacy while realising that this was going to be very challenging for me as an individual and for the family. It meant that Anita and our three young children would spend nearly two months in a local hotel.

The National Party had never come close to winning the constituency and it didn't have an active constituency committee. But those who shared the challenge with us were very good people – mainly professional types, willing to set aside time to get our vote out. We relied mainly on house meetings, although we had two public meetings – the one addressed by Dr Hilgard Muller, the Foreign Minister, who opened my campaign and the other by Marais Steyn, who had just crossed the floor to the NP after being a key man in the United Party. He was expected to provide the firepower but, to be frank, he was a bit disappointing. On several occasions he mixed pro-UP arguments with pro-government arguments. But he did add his basic well-known humour to the mix.

There couldn't have been many people who thought we would win. But we ran an imaginative campaign and it seemed to me that what was important to the National Party pros in Durban was to have beaten the United Party. When I returned to Cape Town two days after the election and reported to the Prime Minister, he said he was satisfied with the performance. I personally believed that a good *local* candidate would have done better – even though we had previously lived in Durban, I don't think I entirely escaped the carpetbag tag. What was important is that, from a campaigning point of view, I cut my teeth in Durban North and although I lost the election, I don't think that fact hurt me politically.

* * *

I have said that we bought a house in Oranjezicht in Cape Town. We did so because we liked it and because we liked the suburb. We didn't buy it because it was the heart of the Cape Town Gardens parliamentary constituency, a constituency which the United Party had won down the years. The existing member was Harold van Hoogstraten, the owner of a local garage. Van Hoogstraten had since joined the Progressive Federal Party but was expected to hold the seat in the coming election. I was not part of the Gardens National Party committee, but as the general election of 1977 came into view there was increasing speculation that I should be the candidate. Whatever the case, the offer was very attractive.

The Gardens constituency extended across the slopes of Table Mountain above the city and included Vredehoek with its large Jewish community and Tamboerskloof, which attracted the crème de la crème of the Cape Town Afrikaner community – advocates, judges, senior business people, publishers, newspaper editors and journalists, and a variety of other professionals. But notwithstanding all this, the parliamentary seat had never been won by the National Party.

I was offered the nomination and I accepted. My official sponsors were Schalk Pienaar, editor of *Rapport*, and Advocate D.P. de Villiers, who after a distinguished legal career (leading the South African team at the International

Court of Justice on the SWA/Namibia case) chose to head up the major Afrikaans publishing house of Nasionale Pers. The sponsorship procedure struck a poignant note. Sponsoring the PFP candidate was De Villiers's son Riaan and, as he signed the declaration form, he paused and father and son looked at each other. One wondered what went through their minds.

About three weeks before voting, I received a telephone call at about six o'clock in the morning from a concerned Advocate De Villiers telling me that the state had acted against about a dozen organisations which were regarded as threats to state security. He obviously expected me to do something, and at the first opportunity I contacted P.W. Botha and conveyed to him my and Advocate De Villiers's concerns and, I am sure, the concerns of most of the people I hoped would vote for me. But my timing could not have been worse. P.W. had toothache and was heading for the dentist. Yet here was this young whipper-snapper protesting against actions the responsible minister had taken on behalf of the government. His response was direct, dismissive and challenging. 'If you can't take this, then resign as a candidate. Go now to Kritzinger [who was the NP chief secretary in the province] and hand in your resignation!' Well, I didn't, partly for personal reasons and partly because it would wreck the NP campaign, to the immense disappointment of the majority of its supporters.

The election turned out to be a three-cornered contest with Van Hoogstraten representing the PFP, Cyril Brett the New Republic Party (the successor to the United Party), and me the National Party. As elections for the Provincial Council took place simultaneously, my running mate was Gideon Horne, a businessman who was also known to be a Broederbonder. So he and I had very little in common other than the determination to win our respective elections.

Although I can't imagine a more fun-filled and exciting election campaign, within our organisation, which was mainly led and driven by Afrikaans-speakers, we had our differences. In fact, from the beginning there were differences between the Broeders and the non-Broeders relating to policy and tactics and who was to call the shots. Dreyer Loubscher, who headed up the constituency committee, was a known Broeder whose preferred style was to run things from a lounge chair. J.C. Krynauw, by contrast, was anti-Broeder, convivial and outspoken. He was also prepared to put his hand in his pocket as far as funding went. The result was that, given an active personal commitment, he shaped the campaign and attracted a lot of young people for whom politics was of real interest for the first time in their lives. This didn't happen through public meetings. In fact, we only had two meetings, one of which was with all the other NP candidates in the Peninsula and was held in the Cape Town City Hall. It was addressed by Foreign Minister Pik Botha, who at that time was the main NP drawcard.

Krynauw understood canvassing very well and he managed to make it exciting. Our electoral office was on the corner of Kloof Street and Camp Street. It was a vacant shop with a large backyard and every Saturday night JC organised a party there to reward workers for their canvassing during the past week and for that day. There was food, wine, music, dancing and camaraderie. Sometimes these parties lasted into Sunday, much to the disapproval of certain conservative members of the team. But it was a strategy which worked, as was evident from our canvassing figures. At one point John Scott of the *Cape Times* called me, wanting a rough opinion as to how we were doing. He couldn't believe it when I said, 'John, our canvassing shows we have more votes than the other two candidates together.' And that turned out to be a fact. The results when they were announced on the night of 1 December 1977 were:

Sen. D.J. Worrall (Nat) – 4,863
H.A. van Hoogstraten (PFP) – 3,102
C. Brett (NRP) – 1, 286
NP majority – 1,761

It was a stunning result. The margin of my victory was astounding, and for the first time the National Party had won Cape Town Gardens with an English-speaking candidate. Three years later the NP would lose the constituency with Dr Dawie de Villiers, a candidate with the highest Afrikaner pedigree: South African rugby captain, Stellenbosch graduate, minister of religion, and member of all the right organisations. What made the difference? Firstly, I was a local candidate. I lived in the constituency. My children went to school in the constituency. Secondly, once the election was called I walked the streets of the constituency, criss-crossing it at least three times and knocking on doors as I went. Thirdly, I had a fun-loving election team going ahead of me and following me, whose spirit was contagious. And, fourthly, I had a cosmopolitan and photogenic wife who was known to speak five languages and who did her share of canvassing, especially in the

Vredehoek part of the constituency.

But there was one other factor in our success which only occurred to me very much later. The reasons I have given are more of a personal kind relating to the campaign and the candidate. But there was an ideological or philosophical reason for our success. The election in Gardens in 1974 brought together *verligte* Afrikaners and moderate English-speakers. I would like to think of it as the first Helderberg.

17

PRESIDENT'S COUNCIL

After my appointment to the Senate I found myself directly involved in policy matters. This was around the time of what was popularly referred to as the Information Scandal. The international marketing of South Africa was the responsibility of a distinct department under the Cabinet ministership of Dr Connie Mulder, aided by Dr Eschel Rhoodie, the head of the department, and other similar-minded people. What they got up to has been described in several books, and I am not going to deal with this here. Suffice it to say that they were not averse to buying the support of particular newspapers and journalists by offering to pay for airfares and buying expensive gifts for wives, etc. In the process, however, they conflicted with the Department of Foreign Affairs and our diplomats, who found their methods unacceptable if not counterproductive.

I became involved in the issue in a curious way. Dr Hilgard Muller, the Foreign Minister, asked me to join him in addressing two meetings in his constituency, which was Beaufort West in the Cape. The first was to be on a Friday evening and the second on the Saturday evening. We would return by car to Cape Town on the Sunday. These were really very pleasant social occasions and, given his obvious popularity, our speeches went down well.

We were chauffeur-driven, so the next day the Foreign Minister and I took turns to read the Sunday newspapers. At one point, and with obvious concern, he drew my attention to an article in the *Sunday Times* by Hennie Serfontein, well known for his political connections. This particular article in effect made the case for a stronger international drive by the Department of Information, suggesting that our foreign affairs diplomats were weak and ineffective. I gave Dr Muller my views, which were centred around the concept of national interest and how it is defined, and what agency in a national or international organisation is responsible for this. And after what I think was a penetrating discussion, he asked me whether I would write up what I had suggested. I naturally undertook to do so. He got it on Monday afternoon after his office had called me around ten in the morning to tell me the minister was waiting for it. It became a working paper within the Department of Foreign Affairs, with the result that I became very close to Hilgard Muller and was sorry to see him retire.

In 1977 the government appointed a commission of inquiry into the constitution with the intention of creating a system of government which was more inclusive particularly of persons of colour and the Asian community. It invited submissions from experts and the general public and was chaired by Alwyn Schlebusch, a senior minister. I was appointed to this committee and it was the first time that I met Oscar Dhlomo of Inkatha, the person most likely to succeed Mangosuthu Buthelezi but who, regrettably, died young. The Schlebusch Commission, as it came to be called, attracted a lot of attention and drew more than two hundred submissions from experts and the general public, only a very small proportion of which it actually processed. Regarding specific recommendations, the commission proposed the abolition of the Senate and its replacement by a President's Council, which in the commission's view 'would be an advisory body composed of nationally acknowledged experts in their respective disciplines drawn from the White, Coloured, Indian and Chinese communities and persons recognised as leaders by their respective communities'. Frankly, this all sounds rather odd today, but that was the reality of that time. What many of us were committed to was moving beyond this and increasingly expanding the inclusiveness of the South African social and political system.

At a certain point, when it was becoming clear the Schlebusch Commission had done as much as it could and needed to be wound up, I put together my impressions and showed them to Chris Heunis, who was one of the ministers on the commission and with whom I always had a good relationship. His reaction was: 'Go home now, and don't come back until you've written this up!' I did so and he passed it on to Prime Minister P.W. Botha. What I proposed formed an important part of the President's Council; and I had a strong premonition I would figure in it when, at a function intended to thank members of the commission, PW shook hands with me and in his clasp there was a quick double-squeeze. Shortly afterwards he appointed me as chairman of the Constitutional Committee.

The chairmanship of the Constitutional Committee, which had ministerial status, was a strategically important post because the occupant, obviously within certain parameters, would greatly influence government constitutional policy. The Prime Minister's appointment of me, probably the most *verligte* member on government benches, to the position therefore came as an unpleasant surprise to right-wingers.

There are many scholarly analyses of the President's Council and whether or not it contributed to a better South Africa, so I'm not going to add to them here. An important part of our assignment was to examine the evidence presented to the Schlebusch Commission, which consisted of 248 memoranda from interested parties in South Africa and internationally. The commission also heard evidence from some 61 witnesses, the transcription of which ran to over 15,00 typed pages. The general attitude which my committee of sixteen persons adopted in its analysis of both the documentary and the oral evidence collected by the commission was one of 'Let the evidence speak, and let all options be open.' We agreed on a particular form in which proposals would be consistently presented and around which their discussion would occur. Most of the preparation work was done by my assistants and me.

One challenge was that every one of the members of the committee, given the nature of their appointment and previous careers, had large egos, and to manage this I insisted from the beginning that we would work on a consensus basis. With the help of members like Bill Horak, Japie Basson and Bill Sutton this approach worked.

18

APPOINTMENT AS AMBASSADOR TO AUSTRALIA

W hile still chairman of the Constitutional Committee of the President's Council, in June 1982 Foreign Minister Pik Botha asked me over a cup of coffee whether I would be interested in taking up the ambassadorship in Australia. The reason he gave was that our representative there, the very experienced John Oxley, had served long enough to succeed as Dean of the Diplomatic Corps, something which the Australians would prefer not to happen. I turned down the offer with thanks, explaining that I enormously enjoyed my work on the President's Council and it was far from finished. However, I asked him whose idea my going to Australia was – his or the Prime Minister's? He looked a little embarrassed and rather disingenuously said he could not remember who had first suggested it.

My committee completed its report with the recommendation of a new constitutional dispensation and shortly afterwards I was summoned to meet Prime Minister Botha. This time the pressure was really on. I held off because Anita was completely against the idea and because I was beginning to sense other reasons for wanting me to move along. At this point Pik once again stepped in.

If I accepted Australia, he promised I would be appointed to London as soon as that post became available. What is more, en route to Canberra he would like me to spend a month gaining experience in our New York mission. Dave Steward, an old friend, who later managed the F.W. de Klerk Foundation, was then head of the mission. Pik also suggested that my family would meet me in New York and then go from there to Montréal, so visiting Anita's family. Then together we would go to Los Angeles, and from there to Taiwan, as the Taiwan government, with whose representatives in South Africa I had good relations, had invited us to make an official visit. And then on to Canberra. This, quite naturally, was very acceptable and overcame all objections.

My appointment, when it was announced, was generally not well received. Colin Eglin, the PFP foreign affairs spokesperson, supported by several newspapers, took the view that Australia was an important enough country to warrant a fully trained and professional diplomat as South African Ambassador. This and some other negative reactions caused Prime Minister Botha to intervene and publicly support the appointment: 'I personally approached Dr Worrall and asked if he would accept the ambassadorship in Australia because I believe he and his wife could make a valuable contribution to improving relations between Australia and South Africa. Dr Worrall considered my request and said he would accept. The reaction of the opposition and the opposition media is that Dr Worrall was sacked from the President's Council. I can only ask when will these people grow up?'

While there were some who thought it premature to move me from the constitutional sphere of government, a very general view was that I was being shipped out to Australia because of a conflict with Chris Heunis, the Minister of Constitutional Development and my direct superior. Closely connected to this was the opinion that views I had expressed about the essential inclusion of black South Africans in any constitutional framework exceeded the bounds of government policy at the time, and that was reason enough to move me along. Rodney Davenport put it like this: 'The government wished to give Chris Heunis additional authority in constitutional matters and needed to eliminate the influence of Dr Denis Worrall, whose indiscretion in suggesting a possible future role for Africans in the proposed new Constitution had also come at an awkward moment.'

A popular cartoon portrayed a commanding Chris Heunis in 18th-century Governor's garb pointing at a rather miserable-looking Worrall and declaring: 'To the colonies!' I framed the cartoon and put it on an office wall and, according to Heunis's son Jan, so did he. Incidentally, while Heunis and I had our differences, these related to minor matters. I liked him and enjoyed his company, which his son told me was mutual.

The Worrall family arrived in Canberra on 15 January 1983. The Embassy, by the way, is in a Cape Dutch style and is identical to the South African Embassy in Harare. What I found to be very acceptable – Anita less so, because I could go back to the office at night – was that a lawn separates the residence from the chancery. So it was that I found myself in the mornings walking across the lawn with my breakfast cup of coffee to the back door of the chancery accompanied by the family dog.

The South African Embassy, like almost all embassies in Australia, is situated in the Canberra suburb of Yarralumla. The site for Canberra was selected in 1908 as a compromise between Sydney and Melbourne, the country's two biggest cities. In fact, Canberra is a fully planned city like Washington or Brasília, and it is not included in any province or state. The suburb of Yarralumla itself is almost wholly diplomatic. The French are our neighbours, the American compound is opposite us, and around the corner are the Japanese and the Indonesians among others. (By the way, the American Ambassador, Robert Dillon, had the habit when he introduced me to anybody of saying, 'Like me, Denis is a political appointee. What's a political appointee? Somebody whose friends don't want him in the Cabinet but to whom the President will give a job provided it's outside the country!' My friend, who had been appointed by President Reagan, owned the biggest Cadillac dealership in California.) With a population of less than 400,000, traffic in and out and around Canberra is a pleasure. And it must be one of the friendliest and most interactive capitals in the world.

The South African Embassy in Canberra is moderate-sized as embassies go. The transferred staff included Annette Joubert, an excellent diplomat as counsellor, Willem Bosman, who handled information, Henk Roodt as third secretary, Aubrey Dwyer, who managed media relations, and a senior agricultural attaché, Dirk Hattingh, given the importance of agriculture to the two countries. (Incidentally, the most important agricultural project between South Africa and Australia at that time never failed to raise a laugh. There is a kind of beetle that subsists on cow dung and it seems there were certain parts of Australia which were covered with dung, and their beetles were just not as good as the South African variety in doing what they were expected to do. And so agricultural scientists travelled between the two countries on a regular basis to see what could be done about it.) Sharon Nixon, whose first overseas appointment this was, very quickly adjusted to being my personal assistant and the start of a lifelong friendship. And last, but not least, Hettie van Soelen looked after internal administration.

Our Consul General in Sydney, which was headed when I arrived by Daniel (Patrys) Smith and later by Tom Wheeler, was the centre point of our commercial relations with Australia. We worked together very well and obviously cooperated in many ways. Patrys was particularly effective in introducing me to leading Australian personalities. The task of the Consul General was not an easy one as the Australian anti-apartheid movement was more active in Sydney than in Canberra. Patrys and his wife, Helen, held many a dinner party for us in their beautiful home overlooking Sydney Bay.

I presented my credentials to the Governor General, the Right Hon. Sir Ninian Martin Stephen, on 2 February and paid my respects to the Dean of the Diplomatic Corps, who was the Dutch Ambassador, Emile Schiff, on 8 February. My staff told me in Canberra 11 o'clock is 11 o'clock and so I arrived precisely on time. He was waiting for me at the front door and his first words were: 'Welcome to Canberra, colleague! Tennis or golf?' I could say 'both' although I was not expert at either. But the Russian became a regular tennis partner as did the French, and the Hungarian and Polish ambassadors became fishing buddies in Lake Burley Griffin. By the middle of March I had made and received courtesy calls from over sixty ambassadors. Many of their countries were not on friendly terms with South Africa, but in Canberra you needed to be friends with everybody because you didn't know whom you would be sitting next to at a dinner party or sharing a barbecue given by a local who didn't take political differences between countries seriously.

Relations between South Africa and Australia at that time can only be described as schizoid. Both countries, in different forms and in greatly vary-ing degrees, had race relations problems which increasingly dominated gov-ernment attitudes towards the bilateral relationship. This occurred against the background of the populations of the two countries having very similar lifestyles and shared interests. Tensions were inevitable especially during Gough Whitlam's premiership from 1972 to 1975. His government quickly acted to dismantle all vestiges of racialism in Australia and adopted a more critical stance in its relations with South Africa.

One of its first actions was to restrict the entry of sporting teams and individual sportsmen and women selected on a racial basis. And Whitlam's successors, Prime Ministers Malcolm Fraser and Bob Hawke, increasingly ensured that Australia was in the anti-apartheid camp in world forums and international organisations. At one level Australia was systematically antagonistic to South Africa but at another many of its citizens – if not a majority – had common interests with South Africans shaped by interest in sport, mining and agriculture and the presence in Australia of a growing number of South African emigrés. In my time as Ambassador it would have numbered around 100,000 but today it is probably closer to 200,000.

One consequence of this relationship was that there was keen interest in what was happening in South Africa and a never-ending stream of requests for interviews and presentations on the country and its relevance to Australia. Australia has a rich communal life with a strong Rotary movement and many service organisations of the Lions, Kiwanis, Apex and Toastmasters kind. Given the invitations we received, my staff and I could have had speaking engagements every lunch-hour and every evening.

Australia is of course a federation of six original colonies joined together to form the Australian Commonwealth in 1901. They each have their own character and we were fortunate in having a budget to visit all the main centres in the first year of my ambassadorship, in most instances meeting with the premiers, other senior politicians, top business people, editors, university heads, and interesting personalities like Sir Donald Bradman. This was the context in which my colleagues and I in the Embassy formulated strategies and policies, and I have to say that we did so without much help from the department in Pretoria.

However, I was fortunate in that, firstly, I had the benefit of those eighteen months in the President's Council, and having absorbed dozens of submissions from not only South African experts but internationally acknowledged specialists in the field of democracy in multicultural societies, I had a clear idea what the issues were. While I was the first to acknowledge our final proposals had a major shortcoming, in that they did not include the whole population, I had a good understanding of the challenges we faced and possible future options. In fact, there was never any doubt in my mind then or subsequently that South Africa was capable of finding answers without the sort of violent revolution that was then quite widely predicted.

Secondly, I had exercised my mind in communicating the issues South Africa faced in an article I wrote specifically for the influential publication *Leadership* before leaving South Africa for Australia. 'Government and Worrall poles apart' is how the Argus group in a widely published report summed it up. And, thirdly, having lived and studied in Nigeria for almost a year, I think I had a sound understanding of South Africa's intra-African relations – and African intra-relations generally – which was something Malcolm Fraser and his successor, Bob Hawke, were both very keen to incorporate into Australian foreign policy.

Against that background I made dozens of speeches to various interested organisations all over the country, apparently with some positive results. According to Marshall Wilson, a senior commentator on the *Melbourne Age*: 'No one can accuse South Africa's Ambassador to Australia, Dr Denis Worrall, of dragging his feet. In Canberra the 48-year-old soft-spoken academic, who has crossed the length and breadth of Australia to put his case, has won a kind of grudging respect from his peers. And while none will go on record, there are many who believe Dr Worrall has made more headway in a short while, than many previous career hardliners. He admits to accepting almost every speaking engagement offered because he sees it as a means of eliciting what he calls "meaningful dialogue" among the thinkers in Australian society.'

There is no doubt that we were getting a positive message across, with Aubrey Dwyer and Willem Bosman succeeding in gaining the interest of several newspapers, notably *The Australian*, which circulated nationally, in our activities. An indication of this was that the Australian Ministry of Foreign Affairs invited Bishop Desmond Tutu (as he then was) to do a lecture tour around Australia. When he arrived in Canberra (and I respect them for this), the Foreign Ministry insisted that he pay a courtesy call on the Embassy, which they arranged.

My full staff met Desmond in the boardroom and, after I had welcomed him, I asked him to open proceedings with a prayer – which I don't think he expected. As a consequence of his visit, I thought we had a case for bringing two appropriate South African politicians to Australia, and I suggested Kent Durr, a member of Parliament, and Mahmoud Rajab, a member of the President's Council. Pretoria approved but Canberra refused them visas.

One thing we assiduously avoided in all public statements was any reference to Australia's race relations problem, which was very real at that time – as my wife and I experienced on an official visit we made to Alice Springs. Most Australians were aware they had a problem and I believe they appreciated my colleagues and me not alluding to their situation – given that Australian government leaders and spokespersons constantly put our problem on the front burner when talking about South Africa.

There was one exception to this rule. I felt it necessary right at the beginning of my term of office to get across a positive point of view while at the same time drawing attention to the Australian government's highly negative approach to South Africa. So we chose an Apex Club meeting in Sydney on the evening of 28 March to make the statement we felt was needed. After a fairly conventional introduction and description of the changing South Africa, I went on to talk about Australia's role in the process. I said that contrary to being creative, constructive and helpful, Australia's policy towards South Africa 'was confrontational, prescriptive and intrusive'.

We had wished to make an impact with the speech but the response exceeded all our expectations. Australia's National Broadcasting Corporation (ABC) has an important breakfast-time news bulletin which largely sets the tone of Australian media for the rest of the day. I vividly remember the announcement on that morning: 'Today Australia's Foreign Minister Bill Hayden came out of his corner punching and his target was the South African Ambassador.'

I also explained in my speech that 'developments in South Africa, which other governments and independent observers had welcomed, had been dismissed by Australia's official representatives as of no significance'. Hayden said my speech 'was totally unacceptable. While foreign diplomatic representatives are encouraged to present their governments' views in Australia, it was not appropriate that they should – as Dr Worrall has done – criticise the policies of the Australian government.'

Reports of the speech and the criticism were carried on radio and TV and in most Australian newspapers. The South African reaction was a mixed one, with government-backing media supporting it and the opposition suggesting that this was the kind of blunder non-career diplomats could be expected to make. Foreign Minister Pik Botha and his deputy, Louis Nel, both phoned me – the latter at three in the morning! In language which might offend some readers, he wanted to know what I thought I was doing. Pik, on the other hand, in a SAPA report, under the heading 'Worrall cannot be faulted', said he agreed with Hayden that foreign representatives should not criticise the host country's policies. But he had looked carefully at Dr Worrall's statement and 'Dr Worrall confined himself to an objective analysis and comment on Australian policy to South Africa only. And having carefully looked at the evidence, I have difficulty in finding words which could more accurately describe South Africa's perception of Australian policy!' This was Pik at his best proverbial ambivalence. I think more accurate was the opinion of Carl von Hirschberg, one of the old-style diplomats in the department, who told me some years later that after that statement he expected me to be heading back to South Africa on the first available flight.

In May 1984 Pik phoned me in Canberra and after the usual preliminaries asked me very directly: 'Did I not make you a promise … for the big time?' Initially, I was a little puzzled but he reminded me that it was an agreed condition of my accepting the Australian position that I would go to London as soon as the London posting opened. I understood later why he offered me London in this strange way: there were other people who wanted to be appointed and who were more senior to me. I told Pik that as a family we were very happy in Canberra and had become very fond of the Australians and had developed an enormous respect for the country.

Donald Horne's book about Australia – *The Lucky Country* – was actually intended as a critique. But Australians have adopted it as a nickname for the country, and they are right in describing it so because Australia is that – a lucky country. Aside from having enormous commodity wealth, its 24 million people live in the thirteenth wealthiest country in the world with the ninth highest per capita income, and the second highest human development index globally. The country therefore ranks high in quality of life, health, education, economic freedom, civil liberties and political rights. And what political issues do arise lend themselves to solutions.

Anita, aside from being very active on behalf of the Embassy and within the diplomatic community, had been asked to be vice-president of the Women's International Club of Canberra – a significant achievement which reflected her linguistic versatility and close relationship in particular with the wives in the smaller non-English speaking missions. She was also using her spare time to complete a postgraduate course in special education at Canberra University.

I mentioned that an important consideration was our three school-going sons, who enjoyed the schools they attended, which were very much like their schools in Cape Town. But there is no denying that London is London and Canberra is Canberra. I also felt that I had, so to speak, cut my teeth diplomatically in Australia. I had made all the expected faux pas, which I hoped not to repeat. I was therefore ready for the big time.

What I did not fully appreciate at the time was the immense honour and the challenge of serving in London during part of the remarkable Thatcher years. Margaret Thatcher had been elected Prime Minister on 3 May 1979, in other words five years before our arrival in London and was to continue for eleven years in what her biographer Charles Moore describes 'as a record unique in the area of universal suffrage'. And I was to interact very closely with this remarkable leader because of her close involvement at that time with South Africa.

So it was that we sent our dog Woden on ahead to spend six months in quarantine in kennels near Heathrow, and began our farewells to Canberra and the larger Australian community. Aside from functions at the residence and in the Embassy, we invited the diplomatic community (which on this occasion included grannies and grandpas) to several specially arranged performances of Jamie Uys's superb movie 'Funny People'. We also invited the boys' schools to attend two separate performances. Because of Anita's many friendships among the diplomatic wives, we were invited along with our boys to spend time in Manila, Seoul and Toyko on our way to London. In all these capitals we were received with great hospitality and warmth.

On a happy note I have to say that we genuinely enjoyed Australia and Australians. With a predominantly Anglo culture, Australia is probably the most successful melting pot in the world – more so even than the United States. It has an intellectual culture which includes brilliant art, literature, music and architecture, and it has exceptional facilities to experience all this. Our visits to the Sydney Opera House were occasions to remember. And it has a good university system. Shortly before I left Australia, the Australian Ministry of Foreign Affairs invited me to choose from a number of books as a reminder of our stay in the country. I chose a three-volume collection of Australian poetry, which still gives me lots of pleasure.

19

A NOTE ON
FOREIGN POLICY

There clearly is a connection between a country's national or domestic goals and policies, and its foreign policy and foreign relations. What Henry Kissinger and others who write on diplomacy stress is the need for balance between the two. In South Africa's case, beginning with the establishment of the United Nations and increasingly in the 1960s with African decolonisation and independence, race relations in South Africa and the government's handling of the issues it raised increasingly intruded into our foreign policy and became a major factor in our international relations.

I was naturally very conscious of this when I was appointed Ambassador to Australia but I think we managed the issues that this raised quite successfully. While getting across an image of a country in the difficult process of positive albeit incremental change, my colleagues and I were able to promote increased two-way trade, investment and tourism. In other words, we were able to do what embassies should do.

London was a very different story. My staff and I did what we were required to do, as the experienced journalist Stanley Uys in his column 'London Dateline' wrote: 'Dr Worrall is a vast improvement on earlier Ambassadors. He is knowledgeable and articulate and has kept his cool in the appearances he has made on British radio and TV, even under rough interviewing.' But rather than being professionally involved in conventional diplomatic matters, my associates and I found ourselves constantly involved in crisis management – crises of our own government's making.

This will be evident in the narrative that follows. And the main reason for this is that the balance between national interest, national goals and foreign policy objectives which I have mentioned was often absent, or the concept of national interest involved was completely mistaken. While one might have expected that Foreign Minister Pik Botha would have managed this, he was part of the problem because he was both Foreign Minister with a clear understanding of the country's foreign relations and, at the same time, the most enlightened member of the Cabinet in terms of domestic policy, and therefore constantly under pressure.

Another way of looking at our situation is in terms of the general principle that ambassadors represent their country's head of state. The result is that the task of an ambassador is made easier or more difficult depending on how well the head of state comes across. For example, I write this at a time when President Donald Trump has described every African country as a 'shithole'. Just imagine how difficult that has made the task of American ambassadors in African countries.

Prime Minister Thatcher met President P.W. Botha once and was not impressed. She also had a number of dealings directly with him that ended disappointingly for the British, something which was reflected in the media and British public opinion and which made our task as the country's diplomatic representatives in the UK so much more difficult. Part of our problem was the lack of a sophisticated understanding of diplomacy and international politics on the part of P.W. Botha and most of his Cabinet. Looking back, it seems that while he appeared to want to change South Africa's internal political situation, he lacked the necessary insight, education and open-mindedness. He seemed to remain the party organiser of the 1950s in the sense that he feared to undertake any change that would threaten the National Party's dominance in Parliament.

Also, the Cabinet seemed to fear his tongue-lashings, so much so that they were prepared neither to advise him honestly nor argue with him. I doubt there were many ministers who understood the problems the country faced or the behaviour essential to maintaining relations with those governments sympathetic to South Africa or the challenges in building better relations with governments opposed to South Africa. And that made my task as Ambassador, in London more so than in Canberra, all the more challenging.

20

WE ARRIVE IN LONDON

The Worrall family arrived on 8 August 1984 in London at the official residence, Highveld, a beautiful 48-roomed house in meticulous condition with a tennis court, a rarity in central London, which was to prove very useful diplomatically. Shortly afterwards I embarked for my office at South Africa House in Trafalgar Square, in effect in the heart of London. I was very pleased to inherit Philistia de Jäger, a very mature and experienced personal assistant who had served my predecessor, old friend and wily politician Marais Steyn. Of my senior colleagues, Leo (Rusty) Evans (apparently, the only person other than me to call him Leo was his mother) was minister, Pieter Cilliers counsellor, and André Pelser first secretary. A very experienced Koos Venter was head of the information section. My first bodyguard was Gerald Watson and then James Fourie, a very able and promising young man with a delightful wife, Matilda. The embassy chauffeur was Martin Skeggs, who really knew his way around London, and who later married Henriette, a lovely South African staff member. They reside in South Africa and remain close friends. Then there were our representatives in Scotland and Ireland, who fell within my jurisdiction.

The best advice I received before coming to London was from Carel de Wet, who had two four-year terms as High Commissioner in London. His advice was simple: 'London is a business posting. You should devote your time and energy to the city and leave Parliament and the politicians to your number two – all the politicians want is a free trip to South Africa!' And that I took seriously. Virtually every lunch time was spent within the City and I seldom turned down an invitation to address a business society or association.

UK business interest in South Africa at that time was strong, as was widely reflected in a story told of how Denis Thatcher who, coming down from the flat in Downing Street, saw a suitcase at the entrance, and asked who it belonged to. When told the name of the person and that he was going to South Africa, Denis Thatcher's response was: 'Lucky bugger!' Also chairmen at board lunches I attended often said things like: 'Ambassador, it will surprise you how frequently around November these colleagues will come to me and say, "Chairman, I have a problem right now," and I would say, "Yes, I know, in South Africa!"' But I could see that the climate was changing: the same enthusiasm was not reflected on the faces of younger members of the boards. And a major blow to British business interest in South Africa was about to happen with what I experienced as the first big crisis of my ambassadorship – the so-called Coventry Four issue.

21

My Connections with Margaret Thatcher

I first met Margaret Thatcher in 1971. She was then Education Secretary in the Heath government and was on an official visit to South Africa. I was editor of *New Nation* and teaching political science at the University of Witwatersrand, and Professor Bozzolli, the Vice-Chancellor, invited Anita and me to a small faculty lunch in her honour. The second time I met her was early on in my ambassadorship and it was at one of several private dinners Harry Oppenheimer organised for us at his Eaton Square apartment.

Apart from teaching UK politics at UCLA, the University of Natal and Unisa, my general reading (*The Economist* and *The Spectator*, for example) included staying abreast with British politics. And in Australia, once I knew I was headed for London, I read everything I could lay my hands on about contemporary British business and politics. Margaret Thatcher's rise to power was obviously a major theme and very early I came to understand her approach to politics (her style was a 'conflict' one as opposed to a 'consensus' one), her economic views and the fundamentals of her position on South Africa. In contrast to Australia, I would be South Africa's representative in not only a much more important country both globally and in respect to my country, but also to a government and leader much more sensitive to both the national and international issues that South Africa raised and the issues in our bilateral relations, in which Margaret Thatcher was the dominant player from a British point of view. This would clearly be an infinitely more challenging situation from a diplomatic, political and intellectual point of view.

When I was appointed Ambassador, Thatcher had already been in power since 3 May 1979, and behind her were the Falklands War, her second general election in 1982, and the beginning of the end of the often bloody mine workers' strike, which began in March 1984 and led to the collapse of labour union power in the UK. Behind her, as her biographer Charles Moore says, was 'the story of the lonely rise of the Midlands grocer's daughter to become the first woman leader of the Conservative Party and then, four years later, Britain's first woman Prime Minister'. That was behind her. Before her was the Brighton bomb attack in the early morning of Thursday, 11 October 1984, which nearly cost her life, and the terror of which Anita and I experienced at first hand. I was an invited delegate to the conference and we were awakened by the explosion and evacuated from our hotel, which was next to hers.

There are many accounts of the Brighton bombing but I find Margaret Thatcher's personal account very vivid. Four people were killed directly by the attack and several very seriously maimed. The bomb had exploded in the room one floor up from her and Deni's. The terrorists had clearly misplaced the bomb.

Typically, at nearly three o'clock in the morning, and still in her ball gown, she was putting the finishing touches to her speech for the conference first thing the next day. Husband Denis was asleep. The security people whisked her and Denis's to Lewes Police College not too far from Brighton, where they spent what was left of the night. She was up by 6.30 in time to hear the first TV breakfast reports and gain some idea of the damage caused – and to begin rewriting her speech. Somebody arranged suitable clothing for her and then it was back to Brighton and the conference centre, where the conference opened at 9.20.

She and officers of the National Union (the voluntary wing of the party many of whom had had to leave the hotel without their clothes though a party official persuaded Marks & Spencer to open early) entered the stage at 9.30. Anita and I were in our seats. Margaret Thatcher then spoke. It was a brilliant address, absolutely attuned to the occasion and delivered amazingly, given what she had just gone through. To quote a passage from her memoirs that reflects the speech: 'As in earlier days, I delivered the speech from a text rather than autocue and ad-libbed a good deal as well. But I knew that far more important than what I said was the fact that I, as Prime Minister, was still able to say it. I did not dwell long in the speech on what had happened. But I tried to sum up the feelings of all of us.'

'The bomb attack was an attempt not only to disrupt and terminate our conference, it was an attempt to cripple Her Majesty's democratically elected government. That is the scale of the outrage in which we have all shared. And the fact that we are gathered here, shocked but composed and determined, is a sign not only that this attack has failed, but that all attempts to destroy democracy by terrorism will fail.'

My term of office commenced with what Moore describes as Thatcher's achievement of a reputation and status on the world stage topped only by Winston Churchill. Possibly of greater relevance is that my arrival in London coincided with an intensified global anti-apartheid and pro-sanctions campaign, which put as much pressure on the UK and Thatcher as it did on South Africa and on the Embassy. In fact, Charles Moore says Thatcher found herself dangerously isolated from some of her Cabinet colleagues, the Commonwealth and Europe but got no significant public support from her greatest friend and ally, President Ronald Reagan. And she was pretty well isolated within her own government, as a result of the position she adopted, and even at odds with the Queen over the Commonwealth and South Africa. It takes enormous personal courage to stand up to that. Thatcher's view that the white Commonwealth leaders acted as a gang of bullies only determined her to resist even more the sanctions they wanted to see put in place.

I understood all this and supported her fundamental assumptions about South Africa and what South Africa needed to do. This was reflected in my actions in London and my reporting back to South Africa. And the Prime Minister and her immediate team knew where I stood.

I was particularly close to Charles Powell, Thatcher's foreign affairs private secretary, and I could therefore get important messages to her through Charles. But the closeness is reflected in a strange way. Immediately after the Nassau Commonwealth Heads of Government meeting, which formulated the Eminent Persons concept, he sent me an important note for the South African government. What was unusual about this was that the message came directly to me and not via the Foreign Office. Powell explained this anomaly to Moore as follows: 'South Africa became one of those subjects for which Mrs Thatcher took over the direction of policy with some help from me, and Denis Worrall was an invaluable source of information on debates within the South African government as Mrs Thatcher and I worked out the direction of policy at the highest level in Downing Street and cut out Geoffrey Howe [the Foreign Secretary] and his officials. I used the reformist Worrall, who had political ambitions of his own, almost as my spy within

South African officialdom.'

When this was first published I received a number of enquiries from friends and others who wanted to know what this really meant. I explained it in this way. It reflected total trust between Powell and myself. He knew what my position was and completely trusted me to get across, at the most appropriate levels, whatever concerned his Prime Minister. And Margaret Thatcher, it will be seen, showed her appreciation very effectively much later in the Helderberg election of 1987.

Margaret Thatcher's opposition to sanctions and her insistence on maintaining contact with President P.W. Botha were highly contentious, not just because she believed the impact on the South African government would be counterproductive and make it even less cooperative, but because she saw they would make worse the lives of the black population who would bear much of the brunt.

This was a time of growing anti-apartheid sentiment and increasing demands for sanctions against South Africa, which Margaret Thatcher almost single-handedly in the West opposed. In the mid-1980s, the Cold War was uppermost in Mrs Thatcher's mind and, as an expression of this, for example, she would therefore make sure of Namibia's independence. She set out her position when P.W. Botha came to Chequers on 2 June 1984, in other words less than two months before my arrival in London. Thatcher's speaking notes for the occasion as quoted by Moore read: 'Good to break isolation – potential goodwill in the West – but cannot be manifested because of the internal situation. Our foreign policy depended on the internal liberalisation.'

Thatcher was solidly against sanctions but equally in favour of social and political change in the country though in a non-prescriptive way. As Moore puts it: 'She felt that reform would only come from within South Africa itself, and that, when needed, the South African government would see in her a trustworthy external interlocutor who could help move it forward.' That was a consideration I enormously appreciated. Whether the South African political leadership or, more specifically, President P.W. Botha appreciated it is another matter. This was a central theme of my ambassadorship in London.

There is one aspect of Margaret Thatcher that I only became aware of much later. It seems that she was not as popular with women as she was with men. This is spelt out in some detail by Mary Warnock in her memoir *People and Places*. Warnock was of course a philosopher and moved in very highbrow, mainly Oxford and Cambridge circles. Her husband, Geoffrey, became Vice-Chancellor of Oxford University. Incidentally, notwithstanding her very evident dislike of Thatcher, Warnock thought it a serious mistake on the part of Oxford not to have awarded Thatcher an honorary doctorate as it had to every Oxford graduate who had become Prime Minister before her.

I asked Anita, who met Margaret Thatcher on several occasions, how she had found her from a woman's point of view. It seems that Anita found her to be very feminine in her interests. Anita says in her experience Maggie was very interested in fashion. On one occasion at dinner with the Oppenheimers, she approached Anita and told her how very much she admired her two-piece outfit. Anita says Elzbieta Rosenwerth, the Cape Town creator of the suit, was very chuffed when she told her of the compliment. On another occasion, Anita had been invited by Sir Graham Macmillan, the Tory Party organiser in Scotland, to Conservative Party headquarters as they were celebrating Maggie's third election victory. They were all drinking orange juice and champagne and admiring the redecorated premises. Maggie arrived among cheers and jubilation. She congratulated her workers and told them to enjoy the drinks: 'But mind, don't spill any orange juice on the carpets!' This is the woman, Anita says, who challenged the male chauvinism of the Conservatives' In and Out Club by breaking the taboo of 'no women allowed' on the grand staircase. They later put a painting of her at the top of that staircase.

Whenever I saw Margaret Thatcher after my resignation, she generally produced the latest copy of *Insight*, my newsletter. It was usually scribbled on and she had numerous questions to ask in response to it. The same happened on the last occasion I saw her in London after she had resigned. It was an extraordinary occasion. She knew I was visiting London, and as she was coming to South Africa, she wanted my advice as to how she should handle various situations which no doubt would arise. So she asked Anita and me to come around for a late afternoon drink. Her new home in Dulwich was not ready and Henry Ford had invited her to use his flat in Eaton Square, which immediately became evident as the cab approached because it was floodlit with arc lights and patrolled by several police guards. Inside, the apartment was completely impersonal. There was absolutely nothing of Margaret but lots of photographs of the Ford family. She had an aide who took notes as we talked and answered the telephone when once it rang. As he answered she perked up and expectantly called out, 'Is it Mark?' – her son. When the aide responded that it was not but some official, deflated she visibly sank back in her chair. Anita and I found the experience extraordinarily sad. As Anita remarked when we left, 'She was like a bird in a cage.'

THE RT. HON. MARGARET THATCHER, O.M., F.R.S., M.P.

HOUSE OF COMMONS
LONDON SW1A 0AA

18th March 1991

Dear Mr. Worrall

Thank you for your letter of 21st February.

I am delighted to hear that your Position Papers are to be brought out in expanded form. I have always found them invaluable and look forward to continuing to receive them.

Denis joins me in sending our warm good wishes to Anita and yourself.

Yours sincerely

Margaret Thatcher

Denis Worrall Esq

THE COVENTRY FOUR ISSUE

My immediate concern on arrival in the UK was with the Coventry Four Issue. I need to tell it in some detail because, firstly, it was an event which had implications for South Africa's diplomatic relations with Britain, for British business and for South Africa's diplomatic reputation around the world. It also had serious ramifications for the Embassy, my standing as South African Ambassador and my integrity.

It is also an intriguing story with several layers of fact and several important players. Excluding myself, who came on the scene late but at a critical juncture, there were André Pelser, the counsellor in the Embassy, Advocate Jan Heunis, legal adviser to the Department of Foreign Affairs in Pretoria, Foreign Minister Pik Botha himself and others in South Africa who I came to realise called the shots from the shadows. And on the UK side, there were Foreign Secretary Sir Geoffrey Howe and Minister in the Foreign Office Malcolm Rifkind and a number of senior officers in the British Commonwealth and Foreign Office. The event was also of sufficient concern to Prime Minister Thatcher for her to require a daily report on it. And then there were the journalists, both in South Africa and the UK, for whom the Coventry Four was a bonanza. I have seen more than fifteen hundred newspaper clippings covering the event, not to mention the extensive television and radio coverage it received.

On Thursday, 29 March 1984, in other words some five months before my arrival in the UK, four South Africans were arrested in London on charges of violating arms sanctions against South Africa. They were Hennie Botha, Fanie de Jager, Koos le Grange and Randy Metelerkamp. They all had connections to Armscor and one of them was a retired colonel from the South African Defence Force. They were transported to Coventry immediately after their arrest, the jurisdiction in which the alleged violation took place, and detained in the cells at Coventry police station. Three British business-men linked to this alleged violation were arrested in the British Midlands and charged separately. A fourth British businessman was arrested and charged later.

Hennie Botha managed to call the Embassy late on Friday afternoon, and was able to speak to André Pelser, who was still in his office, other personnel having already left for the weekend. As my predecessor, Marais Steyn, was in South Africa for consultations and the deputy head of mis-sion, Rusty Evans, was in Scotland, André spoke to senior diplomat Carl von Hirschberg in Pretoria, who advised him to manage the matter as best he could. He took the first train to Coventry, a journey of about an hour, and was able to gain access to Hennie Botha and the other three being held at the same police station.

As Pelser explains, the four were to be charged with circumventing the UN arms embargo which the UK had adopted into British law, for com-plicity in smuggling spare parts for military equipment from a firm in Coventry. Preliminary charges were to be laid in the Magistrate's Court the next morning, Saturday. On Monday, 2 April they were formally charged with illegally exporting military equipment to South Africa. Application for bail for the four was refused by the magistrate on the grounds that the four might abscond, and they were remanded in custody in Winson Green prison in Birmingham, twenty-odd miles from Coventry. Pelser visited the men regularly to show government support and maintain their morale.

Noel Benjamin, the Embassy attorney, arranged for legal representation for the four (who later became known as the Coventry Four) and secured the services of two eminent barristers, Jeremy Gompertz and George Carman QC, the latter widely acknowledged as one of the best legal minds in Britain. Subsequently, Advocate Jan Heunis was sent to London to assist Pelser and the British legal team in the legal process.

On 9 April another application was made for bail, this time successfully. Bail of R50,000, as well as a deposit of R50,000 surety, was imposed for each accused, with strict conditions: that the four surrender their passports, report to a police station daily and be released into the custody of Pelser, who had to surrender his diplomatic immunity in order to stand surety for bail.

Pelser arranged furnished accommodation for them and accompanied them back to London. Shortly thereafter the wives of the four arrived in

London to be with their husbands, one of them with a brief that they should allege mistreatment of their husbands in Winson Green prison. Pelser caught wind of this and stopped this 'stratcom' exercise by Armscor head office in its tracks – because in his opinion, on the basis of personal observation, the four had been treated well. Nevertheless, these allegations were made in South Africa and reported in the South African media, much to the chagrin of the HM Prison Service and the British government.

Following the successful bail application, the legal team explored the legal grounds for arguing that the British government drop the charges altogether. In the interim, given that the trial was not expected to take place before October, an application for the conditions of bail to be relaxed to allow the four to return to South Africa pending the trial would be submitted to the magistrate's court.

Immediately after bail was granted, Heunis joined Ambassador Marais Steyn in meeting with British Foreign Secretary Howe in an attempt to persuade the Crown to drop the charges. According to Heunis, Howe seemed indifferent and more interested in the long-distance runner Zola Budd becoming a British athlete. Ambassador Steyn subsequently wrote to Sir John Leahy, Deputy Under-Secretary of State at the Foreign and Commonwealth Office, as follows: 'The purpose of this note is to inform you that the legal representatives of the four gentlemen in question shall be bringing an application to the Coventry Magistrate's Court for the conditions of bail to be revised so as to enable the four to return to South Africa pending the commencement of the Coventry Four proceedings (22 October).' No doubt Heunis helped the Ambassador with the following statement: 'I have been authorised by my government to give you a categorical assurance, on a government-to-government basis, that the South African government fully intends to honour the undertaking should the court be prepared to grant an application that the bail will be amended to allow the four to return to South Africa given the lapse of time between the hearing and the trial.'

A further application on 18 May for them to return to South Africa was refused by the magistrate, but an appeal to Mr Justice K. Leonard in chambers on 22 May was successful. Justice Leonard doubled the bail, increased the surety amount and granted the application on the basis that Pelser provide surety as he had previously done, and also that the South African government give an undertaking that the four would be compelled to return to the UK should they not be willing to do so.

I am sure that it was with an enormous sigh of relief that Pelser saw the four board a plane at Heathrow bound for Johannesburg and returned to his normal duties at the Embassy. When the four returned to the UK on 25 June to renew their bail, which was a formality, Pelser accompanied them back to South Africa, ostensibly to assist the UK legal team.

At this juncture, Heunis was instructed by the South African Cabinet to undertake further efforts to persuade the British government to drop the charges altogether. It was also suggested he meet with the Bavarian Minister-President Franz Josef Strauss and request him to use his influence with Thatcher to withdraw the charges. When he had explained what the charges were, Strauss's first question was: 'Why didn't you use the Israelis?' Strauss gave Heunis a couple of introductions to persons he said could help, but after two days and no progress in Munich, Heunis flew to New York on the instructions of the Cabinet. The intention was that he would meet with Chester Crocker, US Secretary of State for Africa, with the same purpose in mind. Heunis was supposed to meet Crocker at JFK Airport but missed him. Pik then authorised Heunis to try to catch up with Crocker in London. (Incidentally, Jan van Dalsen, the head of Foreign Affairs, did not know of this activity involving Heunis.)

One further attempt at getting somebody to persuade the UK government to drop the whole matter involved a military intelligence source who suggested to Heunis that Dave Steward, better known as a Foreign Affairs official, should travel to Scotland to meet a person with access to Prime Minister Thatcher. This was, as Heunis says, an 'ultra-secret mission and not even the South African Embassy was informed that they were travelling to Scotland'. Heunis and Steward met a gentleman at Glasgow airport and drove through the countryside while they briefed him on the matter. Says Heunis: 'He assured us of his best endeavours ... not long afterwards Rusty Evans, Minister in the South African Embassy, wrote to the department to say that a secretary in Thatcher's office had been approached by our contact to prevail upon the Prime Minister to have the matter compounded.' Heunis acknowledged that 'Rusty was understandably dismayed!' (I confirmed this with Dave Steward. He said it was 'a wild goose chase'.)

A major development occurred on 21 August, shortly after I'd taken office in London, when the South African Minister of Law and Order issued notices for the arrest and detention of six United Democratic Front members. But before the orders could be served on them, on 13 September they sought asylum in the British Consulate in Durban. Advocate Heunis began to play what was a crucial role in this whole saga when he instantly advised Pik Botha not to issue any statements. To quote Heunis: 'I explained to Pik that by providing asylum to the six, the British government was acting unlawfully in terms of international law. I also pointed out that international law recognises the concept of "reprisal", according to which a valid or legitimate active reprise by one state against another has to be preceded by a breach of international law by the state against which the act of reprisal is directed.' Heunis told Foreign Minister Botha that as a matter of law the conduct of the British warranted an act of reprisal.

André Pelser, who was still in South Africa but preparing with the British legal team to return to the UK with the four to renew their bail, was deeply disturbed by this turn of events. The day before André and the British legal team were due to return to London, he was summoned by Pik Botha, who met with him alone. Pik told him the government had decided not to allow the four to return for trial. André said he strongly opposed this as it would have serious implications for South Africa's reputation in the world, since the South African government, through Ambassador Steyn, my predecessor, had given a solemn undertaking to a High Court judge that the four would be returned for trial. Pik said the action would be justified in terms of the doctrine of reprisal. He also told Pelser that he should not return to London as he might be declared persona non grata and be expelled from Britain. When André asked what would happen to his career, Pik said that the government would look after him. André told the minister that he preferred to look after himself and insisted that he had to go back to London, as he put it: 'I told the minister that with respect, I thought I must return as my failure to return would have serious implications for South African representatives who in future were required for whatever reasons to give undertakings to courts.' Pik said he would talk to President Botha and let Pelser know the next day – the day they were supposed to return to London.

André says he knew Pik was not going to do this and immediately sought the help of Jan Heunis. Late that evening he says he stood by as Heunis spoke to Pik and eventually got him to agree to Pelser returning to London the next day – but the four would not be going with him.

What happens next is best described in Pelser's words: 'I returned to London, went to the Magistrate's Court in Coventry on the day that the four were supposed to renew bail and surrendered bail under the guidance of Advocate George Carman, who invoked the doctrine of reprisal to justify the absence of the four. The magistrate found that the lower court was not competent to adjudicate the merits of the doctrine of reprisal, only to order the surrender of bail. Such an order was given. The magistrate stated clearly that I could not be held personally responsible for the South African Government's action in not returning the four for trial. A gratifying moment was when legal counsel for the British government, Mr David Latham, came and shook my hand after the magistrate had absolved me from blame. He said he was pleased that I had been exonerated from blame for the actions of the South African Government. Hansard records that Malcolm Rifkind, Minister at the Foreign Office, confirmed my innocence in Parliament.'

Obviously, my senior colleagues in the Embassy and I were extremely concerned at the course Pretoria was taking but we didn't know what form it would take, and could only guess at the timing. Against that background I made several calls to Pik, every time urging different considerations as to why the government should reconsider because I sensed the course we were embarked on would cause immense harm to our relations with the British at all levels of society.

On 20 September the South African government pulled the trigger when it requested the British government either to deliver the UDF members in the Durban Consulate or alternatively to instruct the head of the Consulate to allow the South African authorities to enter the premises in order to take them into custody. Following the British government's refusal to comply with this request, on 21 September (one day later) Pik Botha instructed me to inform the UK government, since the latter's attitude amounted to a persistent obstruction of the enforcement of South African law, that the South African government considered itself absolved from its undertaking to the UK government to ensure the return of the Coventry Four.

In that phone call Pik was extremely agitated. We were to inform the British government right away! Absolutely no time was to be lost! I argued back and Pik suddenly said (we were speaking in Afrikaans): 'Denis, verstaan jy nie, Magnus gaan bedank!' (Denis, don't you understand, Magnus is going to resign!) This was clearly a reference to the Minister of Defence and there is no question about whom President P.W. Botha, a former Defence Minister, would back in that situation even if Pik had opposed this course. I realised the urgency behind Pik's instruction: they were afraid that one or more of the UDF members would come out of the Consulate and so nullify the government's reprisal defence of the Coventry Four.

Rusty Evans and I raced to Sir Antony Acland's office as the head of Foreign Affairs. He happened to be at lunch, but we managed to persuade his secretary to get him back to the office and his first words were: 'What is so important as to disrupt my lunch?' Having delivered the message, we raced back to the Embassy to start taking the calls. The South African government had already issued a press release, and the phone didn't stop ringing. 'We stayed with you over sanctions but can't stay with you when you break your word to a court of law,' was the general message from all levels of British society, including many business people.

The South African government's handling of the matter received strong negative reactions in South Africa itself. The chairman of the Johannesburg Bar Council, Advocate W.H.R. Schreiner SC, the chairman of the General Bar Council, Advocate M.H.P. Viljoen SC, and Mr Louis van Zyl, who represented the Association of Law Societies, all protested against the action and sought explanations from the Minister of Foreign Affairs. Their collective press statement appeared in full in the *Rand Daily Mail* of 5 October. Their main argument was that by breaking its undertakings to a court of law, the government had created the impression that it had insufficient respect for the due process of law and this could result in citizens following suit. And according to Heunis: 'For once Pik Botha had little success in attempting to justify the South African decision on national television. He persisted in using a self-help analogy which had no appeal, not even to the man in the street. He would liken the decision in respect of the Coventry Four to a man who threw a stone through his neighbour's window, causing the neighbour to throw a stone through his window. This did not work because the concept of self-help is foreign to all civilised domestic legal systems,' writes Heunis.

Heunis himself shortly afterwards left for London where he would assist Sir Maurice Bathurst, a British expert on international law, in the preparation of their heads of argument for George Carman QC, assisted by Mr J. Gompertz, in an attempt to persuade the court that the South African government's act of reprisal was lawful, bail should not be forfeited and warrants for the arrest of the four should not be issued. Jan Heunis has written more on the Coventry Four and the reprisal doctrine than any other lawyer I know. At the time he was a relatively young man and law adviser to the Department of Foreign Affairs. As mentioned earlier, it was he who reportedly first advised Pik Botha about the possibility of the South African government applying the reprisal doctrine. On his return to London he writes that he found a very different situation as a result of my appointment as Ambassador.

He wrote, 'Whereas Marais Steyn had left the management of the Coventry Four matter largely to André [Pelser] and myself, Worrall immediately became involved, motivated no doubt by legitimate concern about the deterioration in the relations between the UK and South Africa. From the outset he insisted I should join him in attempting to persuade the South African government to return the four. I refused. When his insistence began to interfere with my work on the Carman heads of argument, I phoned Pik Botha. He said to tell Worrall to abide by the government's decision or be recalled as Ambassador. On one occasion Worrall and I visited Malcolm Rifkind, then a junior foreign minister. While Worrall downplayed the issue, I came out with guns blazing. I told Rifkind, a lawyer, that I would bet him that he had in his possession a legal opinion of the law officers of the Crown to the effect that what the British government was permitting at its Consulate in South Africa was unlawful in terms of international law, and that being the case South Africa was entitled to resort to an act of reprisal. Rifkind did not contradict this, but that was the last time that Worrall took me to the Foreign Office with him.'

The court case itself was hardly contentious. Heunis writes that George Carman presented a well-reasoned argument which the state simply did not reply to. After a short adjournment the lady chairman announced the following verdict: 'Having listened very carefully to the submissions made to us by counsel it seems clear to us that, in this unusual case, the four accused are not personally culpable for their failure to attend this court in accordance with their bail terms and Mr Pelser, in that he acted as agent for his government, is not personally to blame for their non-attendance. The solemn promises and undertakings made to this Court by, and on behalf of, the four accused have been broken by the South African government. It seems to us this action must have been taken in the full knowledge of the consequences of any breach of them. That the South African government believed that it had some political or legal justification for so doing appears to us not to be a matter on which we are competent to rule. We therefore exercise our discretion that the security and sureties be forfeited in full.'

That was on 22 October. Heunis chooses to leave the result as neutral. But in Pretoria, the 'bull in a china shop' (to quote Pik's biographer) was ecstatic. The court statement 'was a compliment to the South African government',

Pik said. 'South Africa emerged from the case with honour and without any criticism from the court.' He did not feel that diplomatic relations with Britain had been harmed. While this was Pik's view, it came under severe fire from the English-language press and the parliamentary opposition. In Parliament the Leader of the Opposition, Dr Frederik van Zyl Slabbert, in a very strong statement, said that for the first time he had lost faith in Pik Botha as the Foreign Minister. Pik responded by challenging Slabbert to 'go and look at the families of the four men and look them in the eye and tell them that their husbands and fathers would have to spend years in a British jail – in that miserable climate!' However, according to Pik's biographer, whatever he said was unacceptable to most informed South Africans.

The Coventry court had pronounced on 22 October, and the real cost to South Africa would become evident the next day (23 October) when the House of Commons held a special debate devoted to the Coventry Four issue. The debate was opened by Malcolm Rifkind, prior to which he had summoned me that morning to his office. As he says at the start of the debate: 'I called in the South African Ambassador this morning and conveyed to him the government's strong condemnation of this breach of faith. I also told him that, following the issue of warrants for the arrest of the four defendants, we expected his government not to impede their appearance in court.'

There were several calls in the debate, which involved no fewer than 51 speeches, for me as Ambassador to be expelled. However, the main result of the debate was to increase pressure for all-out sanctions. And this particular debate was one of the first occasions when there were calls for the ending of the UK's no-visa policy in respect of South African passport-holders visiting the UK.

During one of my discussions with André Pelser, he made the point that the South African government was remiss in failing to understand the separation of powers in British government, and the almost sacrosanct role of 'honour' in British society. Once charges had been laid and due process was in play, a political solution became impossible and the judicial process had to run its course. Furthermore, the South African government's reneging on their Ambassador's solemn undertaking to a High Court judge was more than a legal manoeuvre; it was a breach of faith – a deadly sin in the higher echelons of British society.

But what I believe will also be clear is that South African Foreign Affairs officials played very little role in the Coventry Four issue. Initially yes, but once it was established that it was Armscor officials who were held in Coventry prison, that fact defined the national interest in the matter and the issue was immediately elevated to ministerial level where it was to be managed, with the military calling the shots. No Foreign Affairs official would suggest anything so crazy as encouraging Jan Heunis to approach the Minister-President of Bavaria and the US Assistant Secretary of State to use their influence – whatever that was – on Prime Minister Thatcher to have the matter dropped. The approach the South African government adopted also highlighted the fact that detention without trial was practised in South Africa – an aspect on which Labour parliamentarians in Britain focused very heavily at that time.

As regards the Coventry Four, had they stood trial the evidence suggests it was extremely unlikely that they would have received prison sentences but at most a fine, which the Embassy would have paid, and they would have immediately returned home.

André Pelser, in his contribution to the book *From Verwoerd to Mandela: South African Diplomats Remember*, made this very apt observation: 'What astounded me was the power the security structures exercised in South Africa: I refer to their sway over government, their narrow view of the national interest, their waste of resources on propaganda exercises and the way they treated the non-military and state security people and public servants as expendable.' This is completely borne out in the description of the Coventry Four debacle.

Was there an alternative? Yes, we should have kept our promise to the British court that the four individuals would return to the UK and appear in Coventry on 22 October. Aside from increasing pressure on the British to release the remaining three in the Durban Consulate, and ensuring that something like that did not happen again, we would have been seen in our bilateral relationship with the UK and among diplomats the world over to have demonstrated a certain maturity because we had upheld a moral commitment. The fact is that the British consular officials in Durban were getting tired of their unwelcome and uninvited guests whose numbers in any event were now reduced from six to three. The Consulate is small and it was uncomfortable and they couldn't get on with their work. They wanted them out and that was clearly happening. No doubt they would have immediately been arrested, but South Africa would have been complimented on a mature approach to the issue even from persons who deplored its restrictive regime.

Wynand Malan, Zach de Beer and I – three Democratic Party leaders.

The winner of the Wonderboom seat.

Pik Botha – an enterprising foreign minister and a friend from the beginning who, under difficult circumstances, supported me.

Anita and I meet the head of the Greek Orthodox Church in Athens. We were served plum brandy.

With my parents at my MA graduation ceremony at UCT.

Japie Basson, a great friend and the best foreign minister the old South Africa never had.

Anita and I enjoying our 50th wedding anniversary celebration.

Schalk Pienaar – the great editor of Rapport, a lovely person and one of my best friends. *'n Wonderlike mens!*

With fond memories, my two brothers Niel (left) and Terry (right).

The South African Embassy in Canberra, Australia – which was experienced as a great country by the whole family.

Wynand and my first meeting with Madiba shortly after his release in his little home on Vilakazi Street in Soweto.

Chris Heunis and I at the nomination court.

A proud father and his three fine sons.

Colin Eglin – a great liberal leader and a fine politician who, with Zach de Beer, encouraged me to enter politics via the United Party.

Dr. Anton Rupert and Madiba – two great South Africans, both provided good counsel.

Sharon Nixon – my personal assistant in diplomacy and business for 25 years.

David Gant – a pillar of the Helderberg campaign
and one of the real founders of the Democratic Party/
Democratic Alliance.

23

THE RUBICON SPEECH

As Margaret Thatcher remarks in her memoirs, 'the year 1985 was one of mounting crises for South Africa.' Notwithstanding some positive developments on the labour relations front, and the introduction of the President's Council, demonstrations, protests and mass actions were widespread with the government clamping down with restrictions on movement and so on. The result was increasing demands for sanctions. At the beginning of July 1985 Chase Manhattan Bank initiated discussions of a debt standstill and two well-established British banks with significant presence in South Africa began to divest. Their management kept me informed with Marcus Agius, chairman of Barclays, visiting me several times via the back door of the Embassy so as to avoid the demonstrators. The pressure on Barclays came from the anti-apartheid movement and Barclays were as a result not getting their share of the student custom.

Margaret Thatcher in particular and her government were against sanctions. Aside obviously from protecting UK business interest, which had a significant involvement in South Africa, she believed apartheid would be defeated by maintaining contact with South Africa and the South African government and by growing the economy. Harry Oppenheimer put it like this: 'Apartheid is to keep people apart, whereas sustained growth would bring them together.' Most business people in South Africa shared this view.

As Ambassador, this obviously was also my position and I was able to claim the support of three very prominent political liberals who were against sanctions, namely Alan Paton, author of *Cry, the Beloved Country*, Mangosuthu Buthelezi, head of the major black political party at the time, and Helen Suzman, who for a long time was the lone member of the Progressive Federal Party in Parliament but probably the strongest critic of

apartheid within the South African political system. The PFP parliamentary opposition party was also against sanctions, and Colin Eglin, its leader, kept in touch with me on his periodic visits to London.

I have to say I never believed that South Africa would experience the bloody revolution so widely predicted by academics and socialist parties. Given my cultural and historical background I could see the small but cumulatively significant changes that were taking place within white and Afrikaner society – in the churches, in the universities, in business and in the attitudes of young people in particular – although I have to admit there were times when I despaired of the three steps forward and one step back approach of President P.W. Botha.

An important consideration in my and my Embassy colleagues' approach was the fact that Prime Minister Thatcher was South Africa's best friend internationally. She clearly didn't support apartheid but as strongly did not believe sanctions were the answer. We never tired of getting this message across to prominent South Africans – government ministers, top business people, journalists and academics – who visited the Embassy. But we knew she needed to see progress in South Africa to a more racially inclusive society. Our government owed this, not just to the South African people, but to a leader like Margaret Thatcher.

The President's Council in its proposals for the tricameral Parliament had made political provision for whites, coloureds and Indians only. It did, however, recommend a declaration of intent with respect to black South Africans, for which I was directly responsible. As Dene Smuts says in her autobiography, *Patriots and Parasites*, following a visit to London and the Embassy: 'Worrall's notable views included the creation of multiracial local councils and a clear statement of intent about the inclusion of black South Africans.' As chairman of the Constitutional Committee, I formulated this statement and proposals in this regard and, while I was sure the tricameral arrangements represented progress, I sensed a tremendous shortcoming by not including black South Africans in our considerations. But that regrettably was not part of our mandate.

So it was that I welcomed President Botha's appointment of a special committee, which included all the heavyweights in the South African government, to look at constitutional options that would be inclusive. And it was against that background that on 2 August an extended cabinet meeting was held specifically to formulate the government's full constitutional proposals.

A government announcement in this regard was to be made at the National Party congress in Durban on 15 August 1985.

With our embassies all over the world we were told to market this speech as widely and effectively as possible. Indeed, it was Foreign Minister Pik Botha who cast the speech in legendary terms, thereby opening the way to hugely optimistic expectations such as the end of the apartheid system, the release of Nelson Mandela and the beginning of serious talks with major black organisations.

Rusty Evans, my deputy, and I made appointments to talk to the editors and relevant journalists of all newspapers and trade magazines who had an interest. But while we were being pressed from Pretoria to do everything to promote the importance of the speech, we didn't have a clue as to its contents, never mind seeing a copy of the speech itself. What we did know is that President Botha, at Pik Botha's urging, had written to Margaret Thatcher, Helmut Kohl and Ronald Reagan assuring them of the importance of what he was going to announce. And Pik was going to be in Vienna on 8 August when he would address South African diplomats and information officers in Europe.

Our preparations in London included an arrangement with the BBC, which is best described by the prominent British journalist and broadcaster Graham Leach in his book *The Afrikaners:* 'Worrall arranged to watch the speech in the offices of the British Broadcasting Corporation in central London in order to brief BBC journalists immediately afterwards and to appear on radio and TV programmes to explain to the British public the significance of what Botha was saying. The expectations for the speech in Britain and elsewhere were intense. As BBC editorial chiefs, joined by Worrall, listened to the speech in a live satellite link between Durban and London, it soon became evident that it was a disaster. The helpful hoped-for breakthrough into a new era when apartheid would be thrown out of the window was clearly not about to materialise. Worrall put on a brave face, but left the BBC offices that night a bitterly disappointed man.'

This speech, which is now generally known as the Rubicon speech, and which Pik referred to in advance as the most important speech since Jan van Riebeeck's arrival in the Cape (!) and as 'a point of no return', turned out to be one of the biggest lost opportunities ever. Pik was devastated and phoned Peter Hawthorne, a senior journalist, to apologise. 'What can I do, Peter? What can I do to get this old bastard to change?' Aside from the lack

of serious content – although, as David Welsh says, there were some posi-
tives (he calls them 'nuggets of reformist sentiment') – because P.W. Botha's
speech and body language came across so badly, few people realised that he
had in effect scrapped the apartheid 'master plan': blacks in the homelands
that had not opted for independence were recognised as South African citizens and would have to be represented within the common political system.

Barend du Plessis, the Minister of Finance, described the Rubicon speech
as 'a mortal blow' which immediately sent money streaming out of the country. The rand began a downward slide to a low of 35 US cents. According to
Du Plessis, 'none of this seemed to bother P.W. Botha. He kept insisting that
South Africa could not allow herself to be dictated to by the international
community. The Rubicon speech was directly responsible for the greatest
financial disaster ever. We had to pay back all foreign debt – and we did,
to the last cent. But it was heavy going!' Economic sanctions followed, but
ironically enough it was not primarily the anti-apartheid organisations or the
American Congress that enforced sanctions, but Western markets, which had
simply lost confidence in the South African government.

What went wrong? The extended Cabinet meeting that President Botha
called for on 2 August was intended to discuss the constitutional options in
respect of black South Africans. The main presentation was made by Chris
Heunis, the Minister of Constitutional Development and Planning, and was
followed by a debate. It was a well-attended meeting and several important
proposals were adopted with President Botha instructing Heunis to draft a
speech for him for Durban on 15 August 1985.

Over the weekend of 10–11 August the *Weekend Argus* carried a specu-
lative report by Tos Wentzel on the speech to be delivered that week.
Wentzel's source was somebody who had close contact with the Department
of Constitutional Development and Planning, and his report fairly predicted
the speech. It included the suggestion that blacks would be appointed to the
Cabinet. This sent P.W. Botha into orbit. He called a cabinet meeting on
Monday, 12th, where he rejected the speech drafted by Heunis's staff and
said he would make his own speech, which he then proceeded for 45 minutes
to read to the Cabinet, at the conclusion of which Chris Heunis commented
perfunctorily. He was the only person to say anything.

The speech that was eventually delivered on 15 August, as explained
by Marc Burger of Foreign Affairs, 'was flung together in haste. It was a
mish-mash of the contributions of numerous authors with divergent styles

– somewhat of a contrast to the sudden, dramatic announcement the world was expecting!'

Chester Crocker, whom I knew as Chet and as a fellow academic when I was at Cornell University long before he became the US Secretary of State for Africa, in his superb memoir, *High Noon in Southern Africa: Making Peace in a Rough Neighbourhood*, gives some idea of the high expectations the speech raised in key circles. He describes specifically Pik's role in Vienna: 'Pik Botha was at his thespian best in Vienna, walking out on a limb far beyond the zone of safety, to persuade us that his President was on the verge of momentous announcements. We learnt of plans for bold reform steps, new formulas for constitutional moves, and further thinking relative to the release of Mandela. For his part, White House Assistant Bud Macfarlane played along. We wanted to help Pik Botha carry the day. He even offered us a guidebook to help interpret the upcoming speech. But when August 15 came PW Botha fell into the Rubicon he had promised to cross. He put aside the speech drafted for him and substituted his own visceral xenophobia which fell massively short of what was required.'

Within days of P.W. Botha's Rubicon, Crocker says Pik was on the phone to him warning of unilateral action by the South African Reserve Bank if American and other foreign banks refused to roll over their short-term loans. On 27 August, Pretoria closed the exchange markets, and declared a unilateral moratorium on debt repayment a few days later. In other words, one of South Africa's most cherished possessions – its reputation in the financial world – went out of the window. And Crocker blames Botha's leadership for this: 'The President of South Africa led his country into the era of economic sanctions – financial sanctions, imposed not by the free South African movement or the US Congress but by the western market-place, which had lost confidence in his government. Botha had created a panic, and western governments would soon scurry to draw up sanctions of their own, as Ronald Reagan did.'

About the same time Pik made that phone call to Crocker, I got a phone call from President Botha's office telling me that the Reserve Bank Governor, Gerhard de Kock, was headed for London. I was instructed to make arrangements for his arrival at Heathrow. Martin Skeggs, my excellent chauffeur, collected him and brought him directly to the Embassy, and together we went to Rothschild bank. I asked: why Rothschild? De Kock's response was, 'The old man [obviously a reference to President Botha] told me to go to

London and see Rothschild. He will sort things out.' I knew Dr De Kock and found him to be a very likeable person and a banker's banker. (His father, incidentally, had also been Governor of the Reserve Bank.) It was therefore a saddening experience to listen to him explain the dire circumstances that had impelled him to seek advice and help in London.

When he had finished speaking, Sir Evelyn Rothschild called in three or four young and obviously bright officers of the bank and outlined briefly what De Kock had said. They went off and in a couple of hours returned with the debt standstill proposal. A Swiss banker, Fritz Leutwiler, former head of the Swiss Central Bank, was appointed as mediator to supervise its implementation.

In a private discussion I had with Sir Evelyn, as we waited for the proposal, he told me that in his opinion South Africa would have difficulties as long as it had apartheid. 'You must tell your President that.' 'Why don't you?' I said. Shortly afterwards he gave me a letter addressed to President Botha in which in very simple and direct terms he made that point.

Aside from increased demands for sanctions from the anti-apartheid movement, churches and universities, several governments implemented sanctions of various kinds. France withdrew its Ambassador to South Africa; and in late August the American Congress, at President Reagan's urging, passed the Comprehensive Anti-Apartheid Act which banned new investments and loans; and the EU followed with similar measures. But much more important, because it was so intense, was the Commonwealth and the pressure it placed on Margaret Thatcher, especially with a Commonwealth Heads of Government meeting in Nassau scheduled for October. As she said: 'It was clear that this CHOGM will be a difficult one for me.' Incidentally, Thatcher was very aware of all these developments. She had said that the year 1985 was going to be one of mounting crises for South Africa. She was obviously aware of the four months' freeze on the principal of foreign debts, and she spoke of being in contact with her old friend Fritz Leutwiler and therefore knew what was happening.

From a purely personal point of view, the Rubicon speech and its consequences were of profound importance to me. I began to wonder whether being Ambassador in London was the best way I could serve my country. That misfortune followed on the Coventry Four and was to precede the disastrous Eminent Persons Group (EPG) a couple of months later.

24

COMMONWEALTH HEADS OF GOVERNMENT MEETING IN NASSAU, OCTOBER 1985

Prime Minister Margaret Thatcher clearly expected to have a rough time at the Nassau Commonwealth Heads of Government (CHOGM) meeting, so she organised a seminar in September 1985, as she puts it, 'to clarify our thinking on tactics to South Africa'. Aside from Geoffrey Howe, Malcolm Rifkind, Paul Channon, Charles Powell (her foreign affairs private secretary) and Ian Stewart from Treasury, she invited a range of business persons, academics and some MPs who had an interest. She writes that 'none of us would have started from here had we had the choice'. On the one hand the reform process in South Africa had ground to a halt: the constitutional reforms had not worked because they did not involve even moderate middle-class blacks. On the other hand, the European Community was moving towards imposing sanctions.

One idea of importance in terms of developments at CHOGM itself was the suggestion that the community send to South Africa a 'contact group' of eminent persons who would kick-start talks between the South African government and representatives of the black community. The Nassau Commonwealth Heads of Government Meeting was held between 16 and 22 October 1985 and the main participants, or those who did most of the talking, were Bob Hawke, Brian Mulroney, Kenneth Kaunda and Robert Mugabe. The only issue on the agenda was South Africa, and Thatcher stood alone in opposing all-out sanctions.

That she had a tough time is evident from the official minutes. But her own account tells it grippingly, and it is very clear from this that she held her own – at one point, after a series of particularly vicious personal attacks, extracting individual but public apologies from the other participants. The additional mini-CHOGM in London in 1985 was particularly vindictive and spiteful and led to stories about the Queen being critical of Margaret Thatcher for putting the existence of the Commonwealth at risk. The London *Times* of 21 October 1985 quoted Bob Hawke as saying: 'We are trying to coax Mrs Thatcher into agreeing to sanctions.' But, as Charles Powell retorted: 'The lady is not for turning.' At a key point, with the end of the meeting in sight, and to avoid Britain issuing a separate statement the Commonwealth Heads of Government agreed to the sending of a group of Eminent Persons to South Africa to report back on the situation to a future conference.

As Thatcher says: 'This had the great merits of giving us time.' This was one of the options identified at the seminar in September and demonstrates the value of planning and strategising – and, of course, timing. Had Thatcher put 'the Eminent Persons option' into the mix early on, it was bound to be rejected. But it was accepted by the majority as a last resort and so prevented the meeting from being a complete failure.

I have quoted Margaret Thatcher at some length as this CHOGM was a very difficult one for her, and I appreciate this was because of her abiding and deep interest in South Africa. She would very keenly follow the implementation of the EPG through to its conclusion, and the importance of this point will become evident.

As far as my staff and I in the Embassy were concerned, we understood the importance of the EPG. I believe this was less true of the South African government – something I think Thatcher and her advisers sensed. There are several reasons for saying this. The decision setting up the EPG was approved on 21 October. The next day in London, I received a private note from the Prime Minister's private secretary, Charles Powell, still in Nassau. It was brief and to the point: 'Please tell your government not to reject this proposal.' This was quite extraordinary and I lost no time in getting it off to Foreign Minister Pik Botha. Shortly afterwards, to be specific on October 24, I met with Sir Geoffrey Howe at his request to brief me on the conference and the relevant decisions taken and impress on me the importance of South Africa's participation in the exercise.

I naturally reported this back to Pretoria. However, what was becoming

worryingly clear to me was that Pretoria was not responding to the increasing British concern. And so very early on Friday, 1 November, I phoned Pik Botha. I have a very distinct memory of our discussion. It was in Afrikaans and I told him I needed to come home. He asked why. And I said to him: 'Ek wil weet wat die donner aangaan!' (I want to know what the hell is happening!) I told him that I needed to speak to the President. I think he sensed my concern from the urgency in my voice and he agreed that I should come as soon as possible.

I was on the first available flight to Johannesburg on Monday, 4 November. On arrival I went straight to Pik's office. We barely greeted when he said: 'Let's go!' and we walked across to the President's office. P.W. Botha was no stranger to me. As I have mentioned, I'd spoken many times on platforms with him. It was he who elevated me to chairman of the Constitutional Committee of the President's Council, a strategically important position. So I knew him reasonably well. But I was about to have the most extraordinary experience. We were invited to sit at a table which was rectangular in shape. The President sat at the head and Pik and I on the same side with Pik closer to the President than I. Pik introduced the discussion in Afrikaans by saying that I had something I thought was important enough to report directly to him. I started to convey the importance of the EPG particularly to the British and to Margaret Thatcher, when I felt Pik, having slid his hand under the table, squeezing my thigh and leaning forward so that he almost looked up to President Botha, and in an ingratiating tone of voice said: 'Mr President, what Denis is saying is …' I obviously had been much too direct in my approach.

Suddenly, President Botha sat bolt upright, lifted his right-hand index finger, pointing, as was his way when orating, and said: 'She wants us to reject it!' I was stunned and blurted out, 'No, no, Mr President, you've got it all wrong!' It was amazing.

We parted company shortly afterwards but it was an experience which has vividly stayed with me ever since. And the message I took from it, which was to be confirmed by developments later, is that the South African government was completely opposed to the EPG.

Pik writes that shortly after my visit to South Africa and the meeting with President Botha, he persuaded the President 'to allow the EPG to visit South Africa notwithstanding strong opposition from some cabinet colleagues'. But as events would show, the approval was reluctantly given. A disappointed

African National Congress, which had hoped the Nassau conference would produce sanctions, had to be persuaded to support the EPG, which it saw as a second-best option.

Pik Botha describes the failure of the EPG as the biggest disappointment of his career. And I can understand that. But at the end of October and early November 1985, when I sought help, it was clear he wasn't going to promote it. He knew why I wished to report back to Pretoria and his somewhat unusual immediate and positive response to my request may have been in the hope that I would somehow help in bringing the government around. The reason for the general opposition from within government (starting with President Botha) was clearly that the EPG mission was too much like external interference in the country's domestic affairs. This reaction would have been confirmed when the 'eminent' persons were announced, which included Malcolm Fraser, former Prime Minister of Australia and something of a bête noire as far as the South African government was concerned.

Back in London, I knew that the Embassy would play an important role given the Commonwealth Secretariat's centrality to the EPG exercise. I expected the Embassy to advise the EPG on their expectations – what would and would not be possible. We would have an important communication function between the Secretariat, the UK government and our own government in respect of the Secretary General and other officials in the Commonwealth Secretariat. And I believed, too, that the Secretariat could come to play a mediating role between the Embassy and the ANC, which I regarded as desirable. I had met Sonny Ramphal on several occasions at diplomatic functions but was not close to him. After all, South Africa was no longer a member of the Commonwealth, although, aside from the UK itself, we had diplomatic relations with a number of Commonwealth countries and strong sentimental relations with Australia and New Zealand and, to a lesser extent, with Canada.

As regards the EPG itself, it comprised General Olusegun Obasanjo of Nigeria, who was co-chairman with Malcolm Fraser of Australia; Swaran Singh, former Indian Foreign Minister; John Malecela, former Tanzanian Foreign Minster; Lord Barber, former UK Chancellor of the Exchequer; Archbishop Edward Scott of Canada; and Dame Nita Barrow from Barbados, chairperson of the World Council of Churches. They would be accompanied by Emeka Anyaoku of Nigeria, Deputy Secretary-General of the Commonwealth Secretariat.

The plan was that the EPG members would gather in London for a preliminary meeting. This obviously was necessary to determine what their approach would be. And the first meeting I had with them was in Ramphal's office early on 13 February 1986. I had been advised that Carl von Hirschberg, a senior officer in the Department of Foreign Affairs, would be joining me at that meeting. While I thought the whole exercise was important enough to warrant the Foreign Minister coming across, I was delighted to have Carl join me. I knew him well as a very experienced and senior diplomat of the old school and somebody who had welcomed me positively on the day I joined Foreign Affairs before going to Australia. 'Denis, we regard you as one of us!' he had said, which I took to mean non-political and neutral rather than some of the party-committed political hacks I knew of. So I looked forward to him informing my colleagues and me of the South African position and all its nuances in respect of the EPG and their visit, and how we should handle it.

Imagine my surprise therefore when I asked him what our brief was and he responded: 'Denis, we've been told to follow our own judgement!' He went on to tell me that he had struggled unsuccessfully to get an appointment with Pik. 'I only met with him at the top of the stairs when he was going to the toilet!' That was the basis on which we approached our first meeting with Sonny Ramphal and the full EPG group!

The first meeting, chaired by Ramphal, took place in his office. Having been welcomed, Carl and I made short statements in effect acknowledging the importance of the initiative and committing South Africa to supporting the exercise in the hope that it would assist our country to find answers to our problems – in other words, the appropriate sort of sentiment. We took questions. Fraser and Obasanjo were sitting in the front row, and suddenly Obasanjo, to everybody's surprise, not to mention mine, said: 'Ambassador, you were at University of Ibadan and you were the Nigerian one-mile champion!' Everybody looked rather astonished and even more so when I replied: 'Yes, I spent a very happy academic year doing research and lecturing at the University of Ibadan. But I was never a Nigerian one-mile champion but Nigerian Universities champion', and I might have added that I represented Nigerian Universities in the one-mile against Ghana Universities in the annual competition. I would have had to add that it wasn't to any credit to Nigeria as the Ghanaian representative was Ghana's Olympic champion and all I saw of him was his heels. What was clear is that George Dove-Edwin,

the Nigerian High Commissioner in London, had done his homework well.

Obasanjo's intervention did wonders for my standing in the group. I apparently was not a typical white South African of that time. The next day Ramphal organised a lunch for the group to which Carl and I were invited as well as my wife Anita, who had an interesting and very useful exchange with Obasanjo.

Shortly after the lunch, I returned to the Embassy from an outside engagement. My personal assistant, Philistia de Jäger, told me there had been two calls of some importance. The one she said was an African who chose to remain anonymous and the other was from Malcolm Fraser. The African turned out to be a senior member of the Nigerian Foreign Ministry who, when I phoned him, rather mysteriously told me: 'Ambassador, you know that there is a very big African man in London at the moment. It is important that you see him.' Well, I knew who that was and immediately made arrangements to see him. When I called Malcolm Fraser, I half expected the response I got. He told me that, as co-chairman of the EPG and as a former Prime Minister, if he went to South Africa he expected to meet with Nelson Mandela, who, of course, was still imprisoned. The point was made after a lot of buttering up from his side, forgetting altogether how unpleasant he had been to me when I first arrived as Ambassador to Australia. (Much later, when writing this, I thought of Maggie Thatcher's remark about Fraser making himself a very *eminent* member of the Eminent Persons Group.)

The meeting with Obasanjo took place in his room in the Dorchester Hotel. He sat on the only chair, and the aide and I sat on the bed. What was amusing is that the room was full of boxes of plumbing equipment. He obviously used the trip to London to stock up for his farm ('the biggest chicken farm in Africa'). I must have spent the better part of two hours with Obasanjo because the conversation flowed and time just flew. The aide had passed on the message at the outset: this was the Big Man in Africa and, as he was going to South Africa, he couldn't do so without seeing Nelson Mandela. This clearly was not my decision, but I made up my mind who I would recommend to Pik. I knew the whole group would not see Mandela at the outset but, if anybody would, it should be Obasanjo. There was a lot more mileage to be gained through him than Fraser. That in fact is what happened. Obasanjo met with Mandela alone in Pollsmoor Prison, Cape Town, on 21 February 1987. One result is that Obasanjo and I have become very good friends.

* * *

The point has been made that the Eminent Persons Group visited South Africa twice. The first was between 17 February and 13 March and the second between 13 May and 19 May 1986. The fullest description of the EPG initiative is in the official EPG Report, which was published by Penguin. But Carl von Hirschberg offers a concise and to the point description of our role before and during the visits in the book *From Verwoerd to Mandela*, volume 3. He mentions that Pik Botha frequently joined us in the meetings in South Africa itself.

Significantly, the EPG acted as a broker between ourselves and the ANC in London, and we made considerable progress toward shared objectives. So, for example, it was agreed that the ANC and other parties would be unbanned, Nelson Mandela released and so on. But we came unstuck on the question of violence. President Botha insisted on the 'abandonment of violence' but the ANC would go no further than to 'suspend' violence.

However, at an unforgettable meeting with the EPG on Friday, 16 May, Pik Botha was absolutely positive that a formula could and would be negotiated which both the government and the EPG (on behalf of the ANC) could accept. I remember that Friday meeting so vividly. It was completely informal and over a snack lunch with all of us just lounging around, Obasanjo and Fraser included. No speeches were made. It was an open conversation. Pik was remarkably frank in his comments both generally and relating to Cabinet colleagues – this person we will get on our side, that person not – it was just mind-blowing. His confidence was overwhelming. This was on the Friday before a meeting set for the following Monday, which was to be the final and conclusive meeting with the EPG – a meeting which several senior Cabinet ministers were scheduled to attend. This was the meeting where Pik said he was sure he could get final approval for a formula that would satisfy the ANC's conditions.

The expectations were enormous and everybody went away from that informal gathering excited and pleased with what had been achieved. Obasanjo and Fraser left for Lusaka that night to brief the ANC. However, on the night before the meeting, the South African Air Force bombed ANC targets in Lusaka, Harare and Gaborone. Von Hirschberg describes how he arrived at his office early that morning when the phone rang and Emeka Anyaoku of the Commonwealth Secretariat asked the question: 'Is it true

that the SAAF bombed ANC targets last night?' Von Hirschberg says he rushed to Pik's office. The Minister of Foreign Affairs was hunched over his desk in shock. When asked what had happened, he just sat there, too shocked to talk. It is absolutely clear that he had no prior knowledge of the raids.

The meeting with the EPG on the Monday morning, attended by Ministers Chris Heunis (Constitutional Affairs), Magnus Malan (Defence) and Gerrit Viljoen (Education), apart from the Foreign Affairs contingent, was a complete disaster. Heunis, the senior minister, gave a lengthy explanation as to why the government could not accept interference in the affairs of the country and, by extension, the EPG proposals. The atmosphere was as heavy as lead.

The EPG noted that there would be consequences of the collapse of the talks. And, as Carl puts it, we went our separate ways. A huge opportunity to end the violence in the country, to defuse the pressure for sanctions if not end them, was simply thrown out the window by the President and a few cohorts. These are Carl von Hirschberg's impressions with which I completely agree. It was obviously an enormous blow to the country from both a domestic and an international point of view.

For Pik Botha it was devastating both from a personal and from a career point of view. Firstly, he genuinely accepted that the EPG's 'negotiation concept' could work. And, secondly, he had developed a very close relationship with Obasanjo. In fact, he practically said if left to the two of them, they would find the answers as fellow Africans.

The UK and international media responses to the raids were unanimously damning. On 20 May *The Times* of London had an extensive account under the heading 'Gloom and Clashes after South Africa's Cross-Border Raid-Attacks Destroy Peace Mission'. And *The Times* leader – 'Raid against Reason'– found that 'while the attacks on Zimbabwe, Zambia and Botswana may place some obstacles before both the ANC and the countries whose territories it uses – this effect is likely to be outweighed by the diplomatic condemnation it will earn for Pretoria from a shocked and angry world. None of this can have come as a surprise to Mr P.W. Botha.' And in Parliament Sir Geoffrey Howe was reported to say: 'The South African Defence Force attacks on Botswana, Zambia and Zimbabwe were particularly deplorable because they took place while a group of Eminent Persons were in South Africa seeking to promote a dialogue which would lead to the ending of apartheid, in the context of the suspension of violence on all sides.' As the

newspaper reports foretold, the raids brought renewed calls from UK opposition parties for the imposition of effective sanctions against South Africa.

I returned that night to London on the same flight as Lord Barber and Malcolm Fraser. We were seated very close together and it was inevitable that we would talk. Fraser was insistent that this was not the end of the initiative. I didn't tell him that, at that moment, I couldn't see South Africa willingly participating in another such exercise. But I understood what was behind his comment.

South Africa's scuppering of the EPG had intensified the demands for all-out sanctions and, with a number of major conferences lined up, there would be no let-up of pressure on the UK and, of course, on the Embassy. Geoffrey Howe understood this when he said: 'The EPG's negative conclusion on 12 June was the signal for both the international organisations to which we belong and the Commonwealth and the EPG to reconvene, innovatively with a view to considering further measures.'

South Africa's action had caused immense anger and this was evident from Margaret Thatcher's letter to P.W. Botha. 'People will say that these attacks were a deliberate attempt by government to torpedo an initiative which was developing too well. I myself find them hard to reconcile with the relationship of trust and confidence which I thought we had established. I cannot emphasise enough the deep anxiety which we all feel about South Africa's future, if what I believe may be the last chance for a negotiated settlement is rejected.'

The South African action also had an impact on President Ronald Reagan and the US policy towards South Africa of 'constructive engagement', a policy which he supported but which fell short of the complete sanctions that Congress wanted. This intense battle is very graphically described by Chester Crocker, the Assistant Secretary of State for Africa and an old friend of mine from my American university days, in his book *High Noon in Southern Africa.*

My first task on returning to the office would be to manage staff morale. I knew them personally and that we shared our hopes. Then I had to think about my response to the British government. There was obviously the reaction of Margaret Thatcher, which Geoffrey Howe later described as being 'very bitter about what she saw was PW Botha's perfidy in allowing the raids to happen', It meant that the EPG quickly and unanimously (on 12 June) concluded: 'There was no genuine intention on the part of the P.W. Botha

government to dismantle apartheid and no present prospect of dialogue leading to the establishment of a non-racial and representative government.'

While obviously it concerned me enormously, there was nothing I could
do to mollify Thatcher's anger. And as I expected, I had hardly settled back
at the Embassy when Lynda Chalker summoned me to the Foreign Office,
while Geoffrey Howe in a report back to the House of Commons was berat-
ing South Africa for the collapse of the initiative. I also needed to think
about a response to the business community, so committed and so loyal to
South Africa, but desperate for explanations.

SIR GEOFFREY HOWE'S MISSION

For the reason mentioned – my regular breakfasts with Geoffrey Howe at Carlton Gardens – I got to know and like him very much, and Anita became very friendly with his wife, Elspeth. I think Malcolm Rifkind's description of Howe is right: 'Geoffrey Howe was mild-mannered, hesitant in speech, donnish in manner, but combined with these characteristics was a serious intellectual firepower, personal courage and great ambition.'

Aside from the fact that Howe and Thatcher generally had a different approach to politics, they had different views on South Africa – something which became very evident after the failure of the Nassau EPG. I think he had a better grasp of the highly negative response of the international community and of relevant international organisations to South Africa's scuttling of that initiative. He foresaw difficulties arising in the European Council, which was due to meet under Dutch presidency on 26–27 June 1986, and which would be followed by the seven Commonwealth Heads of Government from Nassau EPG six weeks later in London on 3–5 August. And then there was the Vancouver EPG in 1987 and the Kuala Lumpur EPG of 1989, both of which would focus more or less solely on South Africa.

This is why, together with his team, he had prepared a position paper on South Africa for an important Cabinet meeting on 25 June 1986. In it he reminded colleagues that the Conservative government, both in the EC and at Nassau, had agreed that in the absence of sufficient movement by the South African government, 'the UK would be ready to consider further measures.'

I believe Howe was correct in saying that conditions in South Africa

had not sufficiently improved, nor had the relationship between the leaders of the two countries. Although Margaret Thatcher was the only significant leader in the world to try to maintain some sort of positive relationship with President Botha and under very difficult circumstances, I knew that this was not really appreciated on the South African side, notwithstanding my and the Embassy's efforts. In that discussion on 25 June, Thatcher drew a conclusion similar to that of the EPG mission from Sir Geoffrey's statement. It was largely inspired by the awareness that Britain would be taking over the presidency of the European Council from the Dutch in the second half of 1986.

The idea was that the president of the foreign affairs council would undertake a ministerial mission to South Africa, treading so to speak in the footsteps of the EPG. Sir Geoffrey would be the natural leader of such a delegation. Aside from viewing this as Margaret Thatcher's way of postponing any increase in the severity of EU steps against South Africa (in other words, playing for time). Sir Geoffrey questioned the wisdom of such an initiative given the failure of the EPG and South Africa's attitude. And he questioned whether President Botha would receive him.

In the end, following a leak from No. 10, Howe concluded that it would be very damaging, for the UK in particular, for him to appear unwilling to accept a responsibility of this kind. However, he accepted on condition that he was asked by the EC to do so; and his cabinet colleagues assured him they would support further measures, if necessary, in the event that his mission failed.

The programme Geoffrey Howe's team put together included the key front-line states – Zambia, Zimbabwe and Mozambique. The British had initial difficulty in persuading Kaunda and Mugabe. But Pretoria was even more reluctant and, as Sir Geoffrey writes: 'It was only after a strenuous private meeting with their excellent and liberal London Ambassador, Denis Worrall, that President Botha agreed to receive me.'

The month-long visit in July 1986 was one of the longest any British Foreign Secretary had made to southern Africa and the Embassy assisted as much as it could from London. Sir Geoffrey had wished to meet with Nelson Mandela and possibly also with representatives of the ANC and Bishop Tutu. But they declined. On the opposition side he did have the benefit of meeting with Colin Eglin, leader of the PFP parliamentary opposition, Chief Minister Buthelezi, Helen Suzman and others, among them Finance Minister Barend du Plessis and Dr Gerrit Viljoen, Minister of Education. Somebody who

impressed him very much him was Professor J.P. de Lange, who at the time was head of the Afrikaner Broederbond organisation. Aside from expressing liberal views in the South African context, Sir Geoffrey says his (Professor De Lange's) meeting with Mandela had been well received by the organisation's members. As regards top-level government representatives, Howe had two separate meetings with President P.W. Botha and with Pik Botha. Most revealing was one long evening alone with Pik in the government guesthouse in Pretoria. Howe's description of this meeting is amusing.

'We started over drinks, perched on tall stools at a private bar, then enjoyed a most hospitable meal on the other side of the room, and resorted finally to armchairs for coffee and brandy. We were uninterrupted throughout the evening. Pik's mood and tone swung from one end of an emotional spectrum to the other. At one moment, "People say that I'm a kaffir-lover – and I am, and proud of it." At the next, "If sanctions are applied we shall make damn sure our neighbours suffer a damn side more than we do." But he did manage to convey the tensions within the government, between those like him who saw clearly what was needed and those who thought they could continue indefinitely to dictate the pace, extent and form of change.'

The talks with P.W. Botha were very different. They were tense and quite often heated. Howe said, 'P.W. was dismissive of my mission and "would not have received you but for my regard for your Prime Minister". He showed no willingness to comprehend, let alone accept any view of the world but his own.' Howe said his second meeting with P.W. was even more ill-tempered than the first. 'Almost beside himself, he denounced "damned interfering foreigners" and gave no ground at all.'

South Africa was the last call on the mission and I was present for the time Sir Geoffrey was in the country. Based on reports, I knew the mission was a success outside South Africa but I don't think it achieved its purpose in South Africa. Part of the reason I believe is that ruling South African politicians, with a couple of exceptions, didn't understand the predicament the country was in and failed to appreciate the importance of the UK's role in trying to get us out of this critical situation. This was brought home to me at a welcome reception on the first afternoon I was in Pretoria. The reception had been organised for Sir Geoffrey and his mission on the lawn of the Union Buildings. At one point Pik Botha sidled up to me and asked in Afrikaans: 'Denis, what is this all about? What are they looking for?' That the Foreign Minister did not understand and appreciate the unbelievable pressure the

UK, and in particular the Prime Minister, was under in holding off from going the sanctions route naturally surprised me.

In commenting on the mission on his return to London, Sir Geoffrey said the problem was to get P.W. Botha out of the corner into which he had painted himself and which resulted in such intemperate outbursts. As far as Pik was concerned, he sent Howe a farewell note which was quite different in tone. 'I know you speak as a friend,' Pik wrote. 'This we never doubted ... we may still move forward in the months ahead.'

Geoffrey Howe's mission was well received both at home and internationally. At the first opportunity the Cabinet offered thanks at the 'dignified and persuasive way' in which he had conducted the mission, and expressed 'deep dismay' at P.W. Botha's 'discourtesy' toward him – obviously something of concern to my colleagues and me in the Embassy. And US Foreign Secretary George Shultz conveyed thanks from President Reagan. However, there were deep-seated problems in how the mission was presented by Howe and Thatcher's media representatives which were to persist, eventually contributing to both their resignations. But that's not part of my story. Geoffrey Howe, incidentally, was replaced as Foreign Secretary in July 1989 by John Major, whom I met on his first visit as Prime Minister to South Africa in September 1994.

BUTHELEZI AND THE KwaZULU-NATAL INDABA

When I was appointed Ambassador to Australia, it was Foreign Affairs practice to invite appointees to indicate particular persons or institutions or projects in South Africa that they wished to meet or familiarise themselves with before taking up the foreign assignment. One of my wishes was to meet with Chief Minister Mangosuthu Buthelezi and his ministers. But I was quite specific: the meeting should take place in Ulundi, the capital of KwaZulu-Natal, which was also his home.

I meant this as an expression of respect for the man himself and what he stood for. I had got to know Buthelezi well as a result of his Indaba constitutional proposals and my interest from the point of view of the President's Council. On the homelands independence issue I respected the way he conducted himself relative to other homeland leaders.

I regarded him at that time as an important political figure, something borne out by David Welsh, who writes that 'Buthelezi was probably the best-known African leader in the 1970s'. Surveys conducted by Theodore Hanf and his German associates between 1974 and 1977 found Buthelezi was the most admired African leader by 44% of respondents, surpassing ANC leaders nominated by 22%, including Mandela, who was nominated by 19%. Moreover, Buthelezi was found to have significant support far beyond the Zulu people. I also knew his close associate, Dr Frank Mdlalose, who later was appointed Ambassador to Greece, and the very impressive Dr Oscar Dhlomo, who regrettably died before his time.

In any event, my wish was granted, and Anita and I found ourselves staying in Ulundi in what was then characterised as 'the smallest Holiday Inn in

the world'. We arrived by car and had dinner with Buthelezi and his cabinet, following up the next day with wide-ranging discussions. It was an experience I will never forget and I know that Buthelezi appreciated the gesture on my part of insisting that the meeting take place in Ulundi.

While I was not to know this at the time – after all, I was heading for Canberra and not London – I had no idea how much Buthelezi would mean to my colleagues and me when I got to London. Margaret Thatcher knew and respected him, as did Geoffrey Howe and other British Cabinet ministers. His connections with British business interested in South Africa and Africa generally were extensive. He was therefore a regular visitor to London, and there never was an occasion when he visited that he did not advise me in advance of his coming and availability to see me. But he made a point of never coming to the Embassy. We met for a cup of coffee or a light meal in the Savoy Hotel, which is close to South Africa House. On at least three occasions during my ambassadorship he addressed the prestigious South Africa Club. The meetings invariably drew capacity audiences, not – I have to say – because of his oratorical skills (he spoke too fast – Anita usually sat next to him and at his request tugged at his jacket when he exceeded the speed limit) but because of what he represented.

Aside from interest in the role he played in South Africa, he was important to the Embassy, to the UK business community and to the Thatcher government because he was one of the three most eminent opponents of sanctions against South Africa. The other two were the famous author Alan Paton and Helen Suzman. Buthelezi also supported a market economy, which obviously was a plus. But what was of particular importance and of the greatest interest to me was the Buthelezi Commission's KwaZulu-Natal Indaba, which I promoted on every conceivable occasion. The Buthelezi Commission's chairman was Professor Deneys Schreiner, Vice-Principal of the Pietermaritzburg campus of the University of Natal during the 1980s. He enjoyed the respect of all the members.

By 1980 it was clear that Mangosuthu Buthelezi would not accept independence for the KwaZulu homeland – something which, such was the Zulu leader's power at the time, was a death blow to the South African government's plan of establishing a confederation of independent black and white states. There was now an urgent need for an alternative constitutional initiative but the government seemed bereft of ideas.

It was against this background that Buthelezi, with Lawrence Schlemmer,

arguably the country's top sociologist, playing a key role, supported by some very eminent international specialists, sanctioned the setting up of what became known as the Buthelezi Commission in March 1980. The commission, consisting of 46 scholars, politicians, lawyers, educationalists, religious leaders and business people, had as its mandate the task of recon-stituting KwaZulu and Natal as a single self-governing unit, in the hope that it could provide a viable way of breaking out of apartheid structures.

The commission reported in 1982 in favour of the political unification of KwaZulu and Natal in a form of a power-sharing democracy with minority protections and proclaiming that this was acceptable 'to clear majorities', and that there was 'strong and consistent majority support for a market econ-omy system as opposed to socialist or communal alternatives'.

The central government, either directly or indirectly through the National Party, had not participated in the commission's proceedings, and its response was to dismiss the commission's proposals more or less out of hand. President Botha said Buthelezi was welcome to investigate matters that concern 'his own country, but had no right to deal with matters under the central govern-ment's control'.

Hermann Giliomee, who served on the commission, commented on the government's rejection of the commission's recommendations as follows: 'With that, the Botha government squandered its great opportunity to take the initiative in respect of constitutional reform. If it had backed regional integration in KwaZulu-Natal (without trying to control it) it could have sparked similar initiatives in other regions of the country. As a next step, the central government could have appointed duly elected leaders from the various regions to the National Cabinet. Powerful, legitimate black leaders in the regions would have lessened the pressure on the central government considerably.'

This is a very perceptive statement because the concept of regional author-ities could be part of a post-ANC government. And political historian David Welsh wrote: 'The Indaba proposals, whatever their inherent problems were, were at least an attempt to create an opening in an intractable situation ... they showed that negotiations could produce substantial consensus across racial divides. It is possible, even likely, that had the government agreed to the implementation of the Indaba proposals, majority support among all races in KwaZulu-Natal could have been gained.'

These are the seriously considered views of persons – and there are many

more – who were intimately associated with the Buthelezi Commission and involved with democratic engineering in plural societies, which increasingly, out of necessity, took place at that time. I, of course, had also been part of this through the President's Council and what I understood better than most was the significance of the Indaba proposals in terms of compensating for the one big failure of the President's Council, namely that its proposals, because of its mandate, did not include black South Africans. Here was the first serious attempt in a manifestly significant multiracial part of the country to deal with this. The Buthelezi Commission therefore had my complete support, even though it was initially from a distance.

President Botha's reaction was a rebuff which most leaders would have found completely discouraging. Not Buthelezi. As Rodney Davenport says: 'Buthelezi is a very resourceful person and behind that resourcefulness it is possible to see a passionate longing to resolve the conflicts of South Africa.' Obviously, the research done by the Buthelezi Commission, which was more in the nature of a think tank than a committee, was available to be picked up again and, with Buthelezi's knowledge and support, used to resuscitate the political drive that was behind the first Indaba.

So the KZN Cabinet, led by Dr Oscar Dhlomo, got together with some prominent Natal politicians led by Frank Martin and encouraged by leading business people, the process being under the chairmanship of Professor Desmond Clarence of the University of Natal, whom I knew from my days at UKZN. Lawrence Schlemmer, still with the Buthelezi Commission, was joined in this particular initiative by John Kane-Berman of the South African Institute of Race Relations – somebody I've known for years and respect as a down-to-earth and hands-on intellectual. He was vice-chairman. Representatives of some 39 organisations, including the main political parties, chambers of commerce and industry, agricultural bodies, religious groups, and local government organisations, sat behind closed doors for eight months and produced a modern democratic constitution with the purpose of bringing together in one political entity KZN and the province of Natal.

It is not necessary to go into the details of the proposed constitution here, except to mention one aspect which is quite unique right up to this day in political engineering in South Africa. Clearly, as South Africans we have never been able to get away from racially based political and constitutional systems. The Indaba proposals achieved that. The legislature was structured with two houses, with majorities in both chambers required to approve

legislation. The one chamber of 100 members was elected on a universal franchise basis. A second chamber of 50 members would be composed of 10 members each from designated 'background groups': Africans, Afrikaans-speakers, Asians, English-speakers and a group consisting of those who declined to be assigned to any of the background racial or ethnic groups or who did not belong to any of those designated.

This was clever and unusual as an attempt to reduce the reliance on race and replace it with an ethnic-cultural identity. I followed the proceedings very closely, and on a home visit in early November 1986 went to Durban specifically to ascertain for myself how the Indaba was coming along. And so it was that I received Professor Clarence's media statement from the Durban City Hall on Friday, 28 November 1986, announcing overwhelming support for the Indaba proposals. Professor Clarence said: 'The people of KZN would soon have the chance to create a bright new future for themselves and their fellow South Africans. It is my sincere belief that we have achieved a signpost to a new South Africa and it is my hope that this Indaba might soon be mirrored elsewhere in our country.'

That is just how seriously my staff and I took this particular initiative. Our energetic promotion of the Indaba over the months was reflected in the wide coverage in the UK and internationally the day after the announcement. To illustrate, the London *Times*, under the heading 'The Indaba Model for Power-Sharing' carried a very positive and intelligent report alongside an excellent supportive leader 'The First Step'; and the *Financial Times*, on 29 November, reported 'multi-racial government proposal for Natal' and went on to quote Clarence: 'This is a watershed event which holds out great hope for the province and for South Africa.' The London *Sunday Times* reported on the 30th: 'Whites and Indians vote to join new Zulu-led province' and 'politicians and local government leaders are jubilant over the overwhelming yes vote'.

The *Daily Telegraph*, on 1 December, in a report under the heading 'One Man, One Vote Upset for Pretoria', struck a cautionary although obviously supportive note. 'A unique agreement between black and white regional leaders in Natal to establish a multiracial government elected on a one-man-one-vote system is likely to embarrass the South African government.' Its report was otherwise very positive. From the US, under the caption 'Shultz Backs Indaba Plan', the *New York Times* and *International Herald Tribune* reported, 'The US Secretary of State, Mr George Shultz, has emphasised

the Reagan administration's approval of the Indaba plan for political power-sharing in South Africa.'

Anita and I had planned a buffet reception at Highveld that Friday evening, which turned into a celebration of the Indaba. If that weekend there was one ambassador in London and his associates who were on top of the world it was the South African. The bombshell was to come in the course of Monday.

On Monday we learned that Stoffel Botha, provincial leader of the National Party in Natal and Minister of Home Affairs, had rejected the Indaba proposals because in his view they didn't meet the government's requirement of 'effective equal power-sharing without any one group dominating another'. This, of course, came to us in London like a bolt out of the blue. The newspapers, which had so warmly supported the initial announcement, told a different story. The *Financial Times* on 2 December carried Stoffel Botha's announcement under the heading 'Minister Rejects Non-Racial Natal Legislature'. The *New York Times* and the *International Herald Tribune* the next day had an editorial 'The Gods Must Be Crazy, in Pretoria'. The editorial went on: 'This rejection of the Indaba proposals follows a decision by Britain's largest bank, Barclays, to end its South African operation. The bank concluded that the Botha regime is a poor risk, and incapable of moving away from a bankrupt political system.' As was to be expected, *The Guardian* took an even stronger position in an editorial 'Buthelezi's Rejection'. The others all followed.

It was a bleak situation from the Embassy's point of view. And yet I doubted very much whether Stoffel Botha was speaking for the government. Our analysis in the Embassy on the basis of informal connections and communications and gut feel lent weight to this view. Chris Heunis, Minister of Constitutional Development, confirmed it when he said that the government had not yet received the report and would only comment after studying it. The generally reliable South African *Financial Mail* corroborated this with a detailed article under the heading 'KwaZulu-Natal Indaba: Over to Heunis'. And my old friend and respected journalist Barry Streek, reporting from Cape Town to *The Guardian*, wrote that 'Stoffel Botha's rejection of the Natal scheme has not yet been confirmed by any member of the government'.

Against this background we chose to issue a general press release, which was widely reported, denying that the government had rejected the proposals. And as Ambassador, I wrote to the *Financial Times* and *The Guardian*

presenting this view. Although the Department of Foreign Affairs in Pretoria and the Department of Constitutional Development and other government agencies would've been very conscious of the intense publicity which the Indaba had generated, specifically in the UK and generally on an international basis, because of Stoffel Botha's rejection and the controversy surrounding it, I don't recall the Embassy at any stage receiving advice or guidance in respect of what was to us a thoroughly depressing situation. When Chris Heunis did put the government's view on the Indaba in the no-confidence debate early in 1987, it was as clear a rejection as Stoffel Botha could have asked for.

27

RESIGNATION FROM LONDON

I never accepted that heading up the South African Embassy in London would be a bed of roses, and I arrived in London at a point where pressure for sanctions and other negative actions against the country was building up. I was also immediately faced with a crisis around the Coventry Four and the Durban Six. As John D'Oliveira of the Argus Foreign Service in London put it under the heading 'Worrall Weathers the Storm': 'Dr Denis Worrall has been the South African Ambassador in London for just 100 days. By now most new Ambassadors would still be learning the ropes, making contact with the people who count and coming to terms with the new job, a new social set and a new political system. However, right now Dr Worrall is only beginning to breathe normally again after having weathered the most serious crisis in relations between South Africa and Britain for many years.' He goes on approvingly to describe how my colleagues and I managed the issue.

While I knew I could handle the situation politically, intellectually and emotionally, after four years I had a strong sense of having been let down by my own side. As is evident from what I have written, the only sensible way I can analyse my ambassadorship in London is in terms of certain crises. To illustrate:

- The Rubicon speech. The whole cabinet sat for 45 minutes listening to President Botha read the speech that he had decided to deliver, which was an unmitigated disaster. And yet not one of them at the end had the guts to even murmur their concern or disagreement.

- The government's extraordinary and insulting handling of the KZN Indaba. It only fully responded in the no-confidence debate of February 1987. Max du Preez in a report of 4 February under the heading 'Heunis Rejects Indaba Proposals': 'Two senior cabinet ministers yesterday finally and fundamentally rejected the Indaba proposals during the no-confidence debate.' Aside from setting back the reform process, the government's decision had far-reaching international repercussions given the interest the Indaba had generated.
- The deliberate and crude scuttling of the EPG, by bombing ANC facilities in neighbouring countries. The Nassau CHOGM and the resulting EPG sent a warning to South Africa that it needed to put reform back on the front burner. But it didn't happen. There was nothing to counter-balance the media censorship, the repression of black unrest in the townships, and the failure to deliver on the promises of reform to, for example, Prime Minister Thatcher.
- Defence Minister Magnus Malan's short-sighted and damaging involvement in the Coventry Four matter, an issue which alienated in particular British business people because it breached a solemn promise by the South African government to a British court.
- President Botha's inexcusable treatment of Foreign Secretary Sir Geoffrey Howe on his visit to southern Africa, a visit which was intended to strengthen the case against increasing pressure for sanctions.
- My personnel were drawn from the best in Foreign Affairs. They were intelligent people who experienced Pretoria's conduct as an insult. This was evident in the private exchange between Pik Botha and André Pelser about the Coventry Four. Clearly, in that exchange Pik – no doubt under pressure – was completely wrong in his handling of the matter, with a relatively junior official courageously setting him straight.

Against this background, what was clear to me was that I needed to rethink my situation very seriously as it involved a momentous decision.

We took a short vacation in July 1986 on the Greek island of Skiathos. It was not as much fun as it might have been because Anita found me moody and preoccupied and more interested in completing the second volume of Hancock's biography of Jan Smuts. The fact is I enjoyed being Ambassador

but was finding it increasingly hard to justify the role I was being forced into. At the age of 51, I could assume a fair amount of life before me and perhaps there were other ways that I could serve my country. I always regarded myself as a politician of vocation and I saw myself fulfilling that vocation whether as a member of Parliament or in the President's Council or as Ambassador in London. And given the speculation about an election in 1987, my thinking went in that direction. But to make an impact, my involvement needed to be different, distinctive and unexpected. After all, I was giving up a prized posting in exchange for nothing more than a challenge. As my old friend Max du Preez put it in a column once I had made my decision, it was a case of 'victory or the wilderness'.

Whatever I decided would obviously have implications for Anita and the boys. And an important consideration for me was that my decision would impact on my Embassy colleagues and the connections we had built up together. As far as Anita was concerned, she had created a career, admittedly revolving around the Embassy but in a form of her own. She was chairperson of the South African Women's Club and a founding member of the International Federation of Women's Clubs in London. She had written and published the history of *Highveld: The Story of a House*, and she had made many interesting friends for South Africa in London.

The decision to resign was obviously not going to be easy but it was along these lines that I was thinking. However, the process was complicated by a number of distractions in the last few months of 1986, aside from my having to convince my immediate family. For example, I was at home in the late afternoon and was watching the BBC report of the announcement. Lying on the couch also watching was our 10-year-old son Dean. His response was, in a rather questioning tone: 'Dad, I hope you know what you're doing!' Obviously my family's interests were an important factor.

On 6 October Pik Botha phoned me and without much of a preamble asked me whether I would be willing to take up the ambassadorship in Washington. I remember our conversation very well and I also made notes of it. I explained that I would obviously have to discuss the proposal with Anita. But I also told him (we were talking in Afrikaans): 'Ek is polities geestelik laag.' (I am politically low.) I told him, if they wanted London for somebody else I was happy to move along. 'No, no, no. We don't want your position. You are doing brilliantly. The person over there can't make it.' ('Die persoon daar kan die mas nie opkom nie.')

Aside from discussing the offer with Anita, I mentioned it to Rusty Evans. He urged me to take it because he said it would put me in line for the foreign ministership when that came up. We didn't discuss it further. But my mind was made up: I was resigning, something I didn't tell Rusty. And if Pik had sensed any unhappiness on my part in that telephone conversation, he simply suppressed it. I don't believe that the possibility that I could resign entered his mind.

Also about this time Gavin Relly, who was chairman of Anglo American, visited me at Highveld. He proposed that I take over the directorship of the South Africa Foundation, an organisation supported by South African business which promoted South African business and the country internationally. We didn't go into any detail because I told him that, while I very much appreciated the offer, it was not for me. Although I sensed growing support from the business community, with top business people sending me copies of their speeches and ensuring that I was on their itineraries when they came to London, I was sure I would turn out to be too political for them. Incidentally, Anita was present during that meeting with Gavin.

At no time did the ANC officially or even unofficially approach the South African Embassy, and in late 1986 there were no connections between the ANC and Pretoria. So it came as a surprise in what was to be the last few months of my term when Donald Woods, the former banned editor of the East London *Daily Dispatch*, whom I got to know well when I was at Rhodes University, let it be known through a third party that he wanted to talk to me about a very important matter. I knew and liked Donald very much and I saw quite a lot of him in London. In fact, we debated South Africa at Oxford and elsewhere several times.

It therefore surprised me that he was so cagey in his approach. When we met it was also well away from the Embassy. Donald told me that he had been asked by the ANC to explore confidentially a meeting with Oliver Tambo, who was then president of the ANC and who I knew lived in exile in London. Donald understood that I needed to give careful thought to this from both a personal and professional point of view. From a personal point of view I understood that the ANC was and would be an essential part of a peaceful solution to the South African situation. And I also knew something of the Tambo family and greatly respected them.

I would therefore have liked to have met with Oliver Tambo. But more important at that time were professional and career considerations. Meeting

with the ANC clearly went beyond my mandate, and I have no doubt that President Botha would have gone into orbit if somehow he got to know that I was even considering meeting with Tambo; and from experience I didn't think Foreign Minister Pik Botha would help.

As important as these considerations were, I felt a growing sense of dissatisfaction at the role I was playing in London. I believed I could do better for the country, and my thinking increasingly focused on the probability of a general election in South Africa in the first half of 1987. And there was no question that any meeting of mine with the ANC would be manna to P.W. Botha's propaganda machine if it became public, as I am sure it would.

I have explained that I was closely associated with Colin Eglin when I joined the United Party in 1957 and subsequently when I followed him into the Progressive Party. As he says in his autobiography, *Crossing the Borders of Power* in a section devoted to me, 'Worrall and I had known each other for many years.' Whatever faults Colin had as a person – yes, he was grumpy and short-tempered – he was highly intelligent and, as his contribution to his party and the country showed, was a creative political leader. Anyway, I liked Colin and I welcomed him calling on me whenever he was in London as I appreciated his point of view on the South African situation. In his biography he describes meeting with me in September 1986. I remember that meeting but I don't recall the details the way Colin does. I did tell him I was looking to move on but certainly didn't offer any dates or give any idea of what I was thinking of doing. I certainly did not express an interest in standing for the PFP. And I definitely don't recall meeting with Colin in an airport hotel in Johannesburg in January 1987 and asking him about the availability of a PFP constituency. Colin did play a role with the launch of my campaign in that he alerted Barry Streek of the *Cape Times* to the likelihood of there being an announcement around the end of January; and, secondly, he gave Jannie Momberg, who was to be my campaign manager, my contact details, enabling us to start talking and make some essential enquiries regarding Helderberg.

Between September 1986 and early January 1987 I told a handful of people of my planned resignation and my intention to run in the May election as an independent candidate. Among them were Donald Gordon, the founder of Liberty Life, a regular tennis partner at Highveld, and Michael Edwardes of Leyland, with whom I regularly played squash. I also told David Potter, who was MD of Guinness Mahon and to whom I introduced Hugh Herman

of Investec, which subsequently acquired the bank.

Two people with whom I had a very close relationship throughout my career were Dr Anton Rupert and Mr Harry Oppenheimer. Dr Rupert, who was the founder of the Rembrandt tobacco company, which in itself is a very inspiring story, was a very cultured man who contributed significantly to art and music. He also played an important role in guiding the development of Afrikaans business. He steered clear of active involvement in politics but every now and again publicly gave politicians sage advice. As regards our relationship, from time to time we exchanged views. And at this time I wanted him to know what I planned to do. He gave me an appointment to see him in his Stellenbosch office with all its art and beautiful carpets. The appointment must have been for around 10 o'clock and – something that was typical of Anton Rupert – when I entered his office and was about to sit down in a particular chair, he said: 'No don't sit on that one – it is still warm from the previous visitor. Sit on that one.'

I told him of my plans and we discussed them until he suggested that we go for lunch, which I honestly hadn't expected. He took me to his favourite restaurant where we sat in his favourite corner. And having completed lunch, I was about to greet him and thank him when he said: 'No, we still need to talk.' We went back to his office and it must have been around 4 o'clock when we parted. His last words to me were: 'What you are going to do is very brave and I wish you well. But I think *Die Burger* is going to kill you.' The latter was a reference to the National Party's Cape newspaper. My understanding is that shortly after I left him, he phoned his daughter-in-law who lived in the constituency and asked her whether she was registered as a voter because, he said, she was going to get an interesting candidate. Johann Rupert, his son and business heir, who has brilliantly expanded the Rupert interests internationally, made a generous donation to our campaign and organised an influential house meeting for me to address at his home in Somerset West. He also arranged for Gary Player to announce his support for me and to play a demonstration round of golf in Somerset West.

Also during home leave I saw Gavin Relly. Given Mr Oppenheimer's support for, first, the United Party and then the PFP, and the interest he showed in my career and the support he gave to Anita and me in London, I felt I could ask him for some financial support for our upcoming campaign. Gavin agreed that this was a perfectly reasonable request, which we should discuss with Harry Oppenheimer directly when we were both back in London

– which we did over coffee and croissants at the Oppenheimer Eaton Square apartment. After Gavin had explained why we were there, Mr Oppenheimer in that characteristic lisp said: 'But Gavin, we must help Denis!' Gavin and I subsequently agreed that William (Bill) Yeowart, an old friend of both of us and a well-known corporate businessman, should be approached to act as trustee, a role which Bill was pleased to accept.

All the discussions I had with persons regarding my political future were general. There was nothing specific. The only person I recall discussing this with in some detail was the public relations consultant Barbara Bester, whom I met for the first time in London. Given what she did and the kind of clients she served (including Frederik van Zyl Slabbert), I asked her to assist with the launching of my campaign in South Africa. The first meeting with her took place in September in London. Barbara recalls that I told her my intention was to run an independent election campaign with a national appeal. She probably was also the first person to hear me mention Helderberg as a possible constituency.

In the last four months of 1986 I made four trips to South Africa. Three of these had official purposes and the one in December was for home leave. But given my thinking I obviously used these opportunities to suss out the political situation and did so without giving too much away. Although I was committed in my mind to returning and contesting the general election expected in May as an independent candidate, I was not absolutely sure where I would stand. I leaned toward Helderberg, which included Somerset West, Gordon's Bay, parts of Stellenbosch and some of the Winelands. My family had one of their homes in Gordon's Bay and both my brothers, Terry and Neil, and their families lived in Somerset West. I also had a number of academic friends in Stellenbosch whom I expected to lean my way. And Chris Heunis was the sitting member and a serious opponent if, as was the case, I wished to make a point in the election. In fact, one journalist had taken to describe a contest between Heunis and me as 'the battle of the titans'.

I consequently had two lengthy confidential discussions with Pierce Newton-King, a lovely man and a superb lawyer, who had been the PFP candidate in Helderberg in the previous election but who had lost by a considerable majority. The meetings took place high up on Kings Kloof, his family farm which overlooks Somerset West – the first meeting in late December 1986 and the second quite early in January the next year. It was an understanding between us that he would not be too closely associated

with the campaign I was to run, given his PFP connections. Yet he and his family were to play an important role. He was, for example, the person who introduced me to David Gant, who after the election would lead the process of creating the Independent Party and handle negotiations setting up the Democratic Party. And Pierce's wife, Jeannie, and other prominent PFP members played an extraordinarily important role in the boiler room of the campaign because they had the experience and knew the constituency.

While Helderberg was clearly my preference to win, I had to make up a shortfall of around three thousand votes. And aside from the fact that I would have against me the Cape National Party's machine, Chris Heunis had the enviable reputation of being a good constituency member. By comparison, tackling Stoffel Botha in Port Natal would have been a piece of cake – and that was the thinking of several commentators. Even Max du Preez confidently predicted that I would run an Indaba campaign in Natal.

And in fact at one point, after I had resigned and returned to South Africa, I scheduled a flight to Durban to meet with a group of businessmen and sugar farmers who guaranteed the funding for an election campaign against Stoffel Botha or in whatever constituency I chose. The reason they backed me was of course because of my support for the Indaba. I slept on it and first thing next morning cancelled the flight. It was going to be Helderberg. And when that was announced later, this time my good friend Max headed his column 'Worrall: Victory or Wilderness'. 'Dr Denis Worrall left his plum job to fight the Cape National Party leader Chris Heunis in a seat where the NP majority in 1981 was nearly 3000. There are many other seats with better chances than that … A bad performance by Dr Worrall could take him into the political wilderness – perhaps a job as a political consultant or as a member of a think tank.' Well, it was to be neither, and Max was to be the first to applaud it. Gerald Shaw, the *Cape Times*'s reputable political columnist, headed his piece 'Denis Worrall Plays for High Stakes'. But he got my goal absolutely right when he wrote: 'It is a high risk strategy but he is hoping to set a national movement in train.'

My resignation was announced in the Court Circular released from Buckingham Palace on 31 January, and I immediately received expressions of interest and support from members of the corps. The same circular carried a notice of a memorial service for Sir Harold Macmillan, the former Prime Minister that afternoon. Anita and I had got to know him well – Anita particularly well as 'Uncle Harold'. Anita attended it with me and we were

quite overwhelmed by best wishes from ambassadorial colleagues – even the Japanese with 'To new life, Ambassador!' And British and international media on my resignation rated my performance favourably.

Typical was a lengthy editorial in the London *Times* on 31 January devoted to my departure from London and entry into the political situation in South Africa. Under the heading 'Arrival and Departure', the leader read: 'A persuasive advocate, brilliant debater, and knowledgeable student of international affairs, Ambassador Worrall was ideally suited to sell the reform programme to British and international opinion. However, by the time he arrived in London, the political appetite throughout the west was for a much more rapid transition … Also this year has proved an almost humiliating one – a year in which the Botha government has all but abandoned the reform programme, imposed two states of emergency and press censorship of unusual severity, and rejected the proposals of the Natal Indaba for the establishment of a multi-party democracy in Natal. For all his brilliance, Ambassador Worrall could not stem the tide.' And Stanley Uys in his 'Dateline London' wrote: 'Dr Denis Worrall finally departed Britain shores last weekend with many well-wishers wondering what a lone English-speaker will be able to achieve in Afrikaner-land. Make no mistake about it: Dr Worrall has many well-wishers. He was once given a rough ride during his ambassadorship, but even his opponents conceded that, in style and content, his ambassadorial performance was in a class of its own.' That appeared on 19 February 1987.

Stanley Uys was one of those who went on to speculate about what I would do politically and what my political future might be almost before I had left British shores. He envisaged a new political alliance which would provide English-speaking whites with a choice they hadn't had. Other commentators had different views. I believe these are worth looking at given what actually happened in Helderberg and its consequences, among which was the creation of a new opposition party – the Democratic Party – which was the forerunner of the Democratic Alliance, now the official opposition.

After a heavy week of thank-yous and goodbyes, and an official farewell lunch given for me by the UK government, I was booked on the evening flight of Friday, 13 February. Anita didn't come with me as she had to sort out the schooling of our boys and the packing of our personal belongings. The arrangement to take the flight had been planned with Barbara Bester and would get me to Johannesburg early on Saturday and therefore in time

for the Sunday newspapers. The Embassy chauffeur, Martin Skeggs, took me to Heathrow and to the entrance specially for diplomats. And waiting for me was a single reporter and a photographer. I told Martin to stop, lowered my window and gave the last interview of a very busy media week. James Fourie, the bright young Afrikaner who had so conscientiously looked after my and my family's security, accompanied me up the stairs and to the door of the plane, where we embraced and shook hands. He left a note in my hand. It was in Afrikaans and what it said was: 'Dear Ambassador, my wife and I completely understand what you're trying to do and we support you completely. God bless you! James and Matilda Fourie.'

I was shown into my seat, which was upfront against a side window and offering some privacy. And when that plane took off, it suddenly all came together and hit me. And I wept as I hadn't in ages.

28

ARRIVAL IN SOUTH AFRICA AND THE HELDERBERG CAMPAIGN

T hat Saturday morning of 14 February 1987, as the plane began to land in Johannesburg, I was not sure what to expect. Barbara Bester had undertaken to organise a press conference but I didn't know what the arrangements were, and who would turn up. I was therefore very pleased to see a group of journalists and cameramen waiting on the tarmac at the bottom of the stairs to the plane. After disembarking, there was a formal press conference in the airport building itself.

As Brian Pottinger reported the next day: 'The former Ambassador to London, who resigned his post a fortnight ago, faced a large contingent of local and foreign newsmen when he flew into Jan Smuts Airport. Ever the polished diplomat, Dr Worrall positioned himself carefully between the Government and the Opposition. He said he did not oppose the Government nor did he favour the Opposition. What South Africans need above all else is to approach the future in a true spirit of conciliation and understanding of each other's hopes and fears. I have always tried to be a bridge-builder between South Africa's communities and later between South Africa and the rest of the world. It is in that spirit that I approach the coming general election.'

The rest of Saturday was spent with Barbara and others on communications planning and thereafter I stayed overnight in Johannesburg at the home of my old friends John and Lola Newbury. I was told the next day,

Sunday, 15 February, there would be a meeting in the afternoon at the home of Tertius Myburgh, editor of the *Sunday Times*. I understood this would be for senior journalists and columnists. As Jannie Momberg had become closely involved, I suggested he come up to Johannesburg for the meeting. I fetched him from the airport and took him back afterwards and followed him to Cape Town on a mid-morning flight the next day.

The significance of that Sunday afternoon meeting was that it was attended by Wynand Malan, the former National Party MP for Randburg, and a number of his prominent supporters. Wynand, whom I knew well, had resigned from the National Party early in 1987, and as it was quite inconceivable that he would join the PFP, he and his supporters must have been thinking of contesting the coming general election as an independent.

Tertius Myburgh was an astute political editor and he knew he had a big news story in bringing Wynand and me together in that way. But it certainly wasn't what I wanted and I don't think it was what Wynand wanted. Quite deep into the campaign he publicly said the biggest mistake he had made was to link up with me. But I will revert to this presently.

The main thrust of media speculation both immediately prior to my returning to South Africa and after that weekend was what constituency I was going to contest. Most reports suggested I would run an Indaba campaign, given that this had been a preoccupation in my last weeks at the Embassy. It was likely therefore, so the speculation went, to be a KZN seat, and most probably Port Natal, the constituency of Stoffel Botha, leader of the National Party in that province. This view was very strongly punted by, among others, the well-known columnist Max du Preez. There were references to Helderberg and my opposing the sitting member and Cape NP leader, Chris Heunis. But no journalist pressed it too hard, I think very largely because it was thought to be an impossible undertaking which I was neither stupid nor ambitious enough to pursue. In fact, after I made the decision to go for Helderberg, two of the top political journalists in Cape Town combined to write a prominently placed article under the heading 'Has Worrall Bitten Off More than He Can Chew?' The journalists were Barry Streek and Anthony Johnson, and their article appeared in the *Cape Times* of 28 March.

'Dr Denis Worrall has taken to striding majestically into election meetings with his entourage to the goose-pimply strains of Vangelis' film score for "Chariots of Fire". The audience, charged with emotion, rise to applaud the great white hope of South African politics who returned home so

dramatically a month earlier to take on the might of the Cape National Party.

'But despite the glamour and glitz of Dr Denis Worrall's campaign in Helderberg, the hard reality is that he may have bitten off more than he can chew in trying to pull off the election upset of South Africa's political history. In the end, elections are not won by the big crowds, innovative videos, catchy bumper stickers or splash press coverage, but by the number of votes cast on polling day. To get those crosses placed on or before May 6 by the 21,649 voters in the constituency does involve enthusiasm for a cause or for a candidate. But, probably more important, it involves organization, not just on the polling day, but for months and years beforehand.

'The old saying "Elections are won on perspiration, not inspiration" does not bode well for the newcomer in the Helderberg fight. And seasoned political observers are convinced that this is where the buoyant Worrall campaign is coming unstuck.' The article carried a photograph of me with the caption 'No job'. Streek and Johnson were two of the first journalists to congratulate me in print after the election result in Helderberg was announced.

The reality is that over that first weekend back in South Africa I hadn't made up my mind. I wanted it to be Helderberg. That's where the real challenge lay. So after deciding early on the Monday to turn down the offer to contest Durban Point, I met Jannie Momberg and his wife, Trienie, that afternoon. Jannie, as I have explained, was a prominent but disillusioned member of the National Party and was looking for a new political home. He had farmed in the constituency and knew it extremely well, including all the power players. He was also one of the first persons to urge me to stand in Helderberg. That afternoon Jannie became pivotal to the campaign. As he says in his biography, he didn't have time for any regrets about leaving the National Party because the next day (Wednesday) I announced my candidacy in Helderberg at a press conference. And as Jannie writes: 'It was a huge turnout of journalists and it was soon evident that this was going to be the election that would have the most interest in the coming General Election on 6 May.'

After the euphoria of the press conference, reality hit us. At that point we were just two people who had taken on the mighty, well-oiled Cape National Party machine. We didn't have an office or furniture or volunteers. As a starter, and very much against his will, Jannie contacted the PFP constituency chairperson, Pierce Newton-King, and got the names of the best and most experienced PFP election workers (the PFP had made it clear that they

would not put up a candidate in the constituency where I chose to stand). As for offices we settled on two, both close to each other on Main Road which runs through the centre of Somerset West. The principal office, an old vacant shop, would be where I would hang out and would also house our media section. Jannie's office, which effectively was the boiler room of the campaign, was on the first floor of an old house also on Main Road. That's where the special and postal votes were managed, house meetings organised, and from where canvassers emerged every night, returning later with completed canvassing cards – the gold in any election campaign – to be eagerly scanned and assessed the next day – so many for us, so many against us, and so many uncertain or not voting.

Our organisation grew dramatically following a packed meeting of fifteen hundred in the Stellenbosch City Hall on 26 March 1987. The meeting was covered by six international television stations and naturally by all leading South African media groups. The meeting drew people like Dave Gant, the farmer and industrialist, Keith Gurney, Alan Tamaris, Chris Reader, the advertising executive, and Wrench Louw, one of the top farmers in the area; and many others came forward. Gary Player, the famous South African golfer, specially flew down from Johannesburg to be present at the meeting and to publicly declare his support for me and what I stood for.

Dave Gant, who was to play a critical role in the Helderberg campaign and subsequently in the creation of the Independent Party and in negotiations setting up the Democratic Party (the forerunner of the Democratic Alliance), described his political involvement like this: he was interested in politics but was not directly involved. Neither the PFP nor the National Party attracted him, but after the Rubicon speech, which hit his business hard, as it did many mid-sized businesses, he decided to act. 'The Rubicon Speech disillusioned me and heightened my resolve to get actively involved in politics and my chance came when Dr Denis Worrall dramatically resigned as the South African Ambassador to the Court of St James, and elected to stand in the Helderberg Constituency. His "independent" candidacy allowed me and others to respond to something new and unblemished and provided us with the political beacon we could follow, casting aside old prejudices and tradition.' Shortly after my arrival in South Africa, Pierce Newton-King introduced me to David. Aside from being a key adviser and decision-maker, he undertook as his immediate task the raising of funds.

After the meeting at which I announced my candidacy, we placed an

advertisement in the local *District Mail* calling for volunteer workers, and they came in their droves. Jannie handled this and we almost immediately had a full election team with Viv Zaayman as election agent and Jeannie Newton-King taking charge of street campaigning. Gloria Woodland was in charge of special and postal votes, and Sheila Harvey became my secretary.

As regards the media, we had the benefit of a highly reputable journalist, Sybelle Albrecht, who rapidly gained a reputation for the Worrall campaign as being faster than the Heunis team in getting our stories to the media. The campaign quickly got into gear, but Jannie tells of how, when they held their first strategy meeting, 'I became quite irritated by a little woman who kept interrupting me. Exasperated, I asked: Excuse me, but who are you? She replied, Dr Anita Worrall.' Anita participated very fully in the Helderberg campaign once she and the boys had joined me from London.

We had a number of public meetings, only two of which were out of the constituency. The one organised by Barbara Bester was in the Blue Restaurant on Johannesburg Station and was actually a meeting of the Johannesburg Press Club with a record turnout of over 180 members, according to newspaper reports. The other was an address to the Durban Club, which was organised by Dr Robert Hall, an American dentistry specialist who had retired to a farm in the Stellenbosch area. The Durban meeting was a deliberate fundraising venture. Dr Hall accompanied and introduced me. I don't know how much money we raised from the meeting but I do know the Durban Jewish community were very generous in support of my campaign.

Johann Rupert took it upon himself to persuade Gary Player to make a second visit and to play a demonstration round of golf on the Somerset West course. I played the round with him but, as Jannie writes, 'I was truly thankful that the voters did not see their candidate play golf, as it would have spelt disaster!' That evening one of the relatively young but prominent farmers in Stellenbosch, Braam van Velden, hosted a braai on his farm and a large number of farmers turned up, probably more to meet Gary than to listen to me. The media coverage that Gary's support generated was amazing. We have remained friends ever since.

The public meetings in the constituency, which Jannie addressed with me, were organised by Koos Myburgh. Our signature tune was the stirring music from 'Chariots of Fire' (I later learnt this was a favourite of Margaret Thatcher). As this played, Koos would give the signal and the meeting chairman, Jannie and I would stride into the almost invariably packed hall.

Although public meetings were where we got our message across to what was in effect a South African audience, much more effective in winning votes were the house meetings we organised. We devised a unique system at the time to see as many voters as we could in an evening. I taped two videos, in which important aspects of our policy would be put to me by two well-known media personalities. The English interviewer was the journalist Harald Pakendorf and the Afrikaans former editor of *Rapport* newspaper, Dr Willem de Klerk, older brother of F.W.

The strategy worked like this. We would decide on a street or streets to be canvassed, and at 6 o'clock I would address a house meeting of up to twenty people, answering questions when necessary. While I was busy at this meeting, one of the canvassers would go to another house in the street where there were also about twenty people, and play the video. As the video finished, I would walk in and answer any outstanding questions. Meanwhile, the canvasser would go to another house meeting and play the video. Using this system, we managed to meet almost a hundred voters in an evening.

Some people who offered their homes for house meetings would go to a lot of trouble by providing snacks and drinks. It wasn't expected of them. One of the biggest house meetings was at Johann Rupert's home. He assisted the campaign in various ways, so encouraging leading business people to support me. And on nomination day Jannie managed to achieve a shock surprise for the Heunis camp when he persuaded Wrench Louw – a very prominent farmer – to nominate me. As Jannie says, this sent shock waves through the Heunis camp as Louw was very influential in Stellenbosch. Among those who, following the nomination, offered their assistance were Jan 'Boland' Coetzee and Hempies du Toit, both rugby Springboks and well-known wine farmers who assisted us in bringing out the vote on election day.

The Helderberg campaign was the focal point of interest in the May 1987 general election. This was guaranteed by both national and international publicity. My colleagues and I promoted an end to all discrimination, the scrapping of the Group Areas Act, the unbanning of political parties, the release of political prisoners and open-ended negotiations towards a new democratic constitution for all South Africans. While this was exceptional, it wasn't what attracted the support I got in the Helderberg constituency and from across the country and internationally. What was unique was the personal circumstances of my candidature, as conveyed by the media.

The editorial in the London *Independent* claimed: 'Not only has South

Africa lost the most eloquent advocate it has ever had in Britain, but the foremost English-speaking member of President Botha's National Party is now in opposition.' 'Breaking the Mould of White Politics' was the heading of a *Sunday Times* article by Stanley Uys in London. 'The resignation of Dr Denis Worrall as South Africa's Ambassador in Britain has been big news here. Most newspapers published it on their front pages and it was top of many television and radio bulletins ... The event showed how passionately interested Britain still is in South Africa,' Uys wrote. And Cliff Scott, the Argus Group's representative in London, headed his report 'Denis Worrall: Coming Home to Build Bridges' and wrote: 'Denis Worrall sat in his pan-elled office overlooking Trafalgar Square two short hours after the storm had broken over his resignation as Ambassador to London ... He was in the middle of a crisis, a South African convinced that this was a time for building bridges between white and black. Feeling so strongly about it that he is prepared to scrap his really quite distinguished career as a diplomat and take his chances again in the turbulent and often ugly cockpit of South African politics.'

The point I'm making is that statements like these created a nation-wide climate ready for a message of radical change. Over and over again I repeated the refrain: 'By voting for me you are not going to change the government. But you are going to send the government a message – a powerful message – White South Africans are ready for change!' What was evident from the closeness of the eventual election result – remember, 20 votes out of more than 18,000 cast made the difference – was that there was a high level of support from all over the country and from both main language groups for the Helderberg platform. Expressed differently, white South Africans were ready for change and did not want to be painted into a 'white minority' corner such as had been the case in Rhodesia/Zimbabwe.

As was very clear, my decision to resign the ambassadorship and return to South Africa and enter the political fray was widely and generally reported in positive terms. So too was the announcement of my candidacy in the Helderberg constituency. Shortly after this Anita, who it will be recalled had to stay on in London for a while to sort out the boys' schooling and orga-nise the packing of our personal possessions, received a phone call from a Conservative member of Parliament who said he had something confidential to discuss with her. This was followed by a visit to Highveld of two MPs who told Anita their visit was on the instruction of Prime Minister Thatcher,

who wanted to help me in the election, given the role I had played when I was in London. It was therefore an expression of appreciation on her part. However, she naturally understood that it was essential that I should approve her proposal which was that she would make it possible for Sir Graham Macmillan, the Conservative Party's chief organiser in Scotland, to join my election team. Naturally, this would all be done on a confidential basis.

It was not an easy decision to make and initially it remained between Anita and me but later involved Dave Gant and Jannie Momberg. There was no doubt in our minds that having Sir Graham as part of the campaign would be an enormous advantage. After all, the UK has the oldest Parliament with a highly developed electoral and political party system. We felt sure Sir Graham would enrich our campaign even working from a back office. But we didn't think his presence could be kept a secret for too long. Quite frankly, I wasn't worried about Margaret Thatcher's reaction. She knew me, and she knew that I was fighting P.W. Botha, who, frankly, was somebody she didn't care for. As regards the National Party, I didn't doubt it would go ballistic. I also didn't doubt that strong supporters of the National Party would react negatively. But the individual voters we were looking for was people who would know of Margaret Thatcher's strong opposition to sanctions against South Africa and who would therefore cheer her support for my candidature. So Anita conveyed this message to her contacts: 'Please thank the Prime Minister for this much appreciated supportive gesture. We look forward to receiving Sir Graham in Helderberg.'

We knew him to be a silver-haired mustachioed gentleman of around 60 years with a great sense of humour and oodles of charm. Once he was installed, he delighted everybody around him. We organised accommodation for him in the constituency, arranged for him to have a car, and gave him an office where Jannie held out in what had appropriately become known as 'the Beehive', as that was where the action was. Sir Graham, a highly convivial person, was only too keen to share his immense knowledge of elections and electioneering with his co-workers. As Jeannie Newton-King, who was in charge of street campaigning, says of him: 'Most of us had fought elections before but this was a very different kind of campaign. It was different because of the candidate's commitment and because of Sir Graham's presence. His response to the ups and downs of the campaign were just different, as was his humour.'

Although we didn't advertise Sir Graham's involvement – for example,

he was not mentioned anywhere and he was inconspicuous in the audience at public meetings – it was inevitable that the National Party would come to know of his involvement. And how that happened is in itself an interesting story. On 26 March 1987 several newspapers carried a report of a political speech President P.W. Botha made the previous night in Ermelo in the Transvaal attacking me as 'the British industry's candidate' in the election. He repeated the charge several times after that. What intrigued me was his coupling of me to British industry. So I asked Sir Graham to explain to me in detail how he was approached and to tell me what arrangements were made regarding his travel plans and so on. He said he travelled to South Africa by SAA. Did he know who paid for the ticket? Yes, he thought it was the British South Africa Chamber of Industry! South Africa's spooks in London could not have had an easier assignment! The British industry connection was to persist right down to the last hours of the campaign. At the announcement of the result, when the electoral officer declared the election a victory for my opponent by a tiny margin, in his victory statement Chris Heunis said this represented 'a victory over overseas funding'.

Aside from Sir Graham's input, I don't doubt that Prime Minister Thatcher's indirect but highly publicised association with my campaign contributed significantly to that extraordinary outcome and, more importantly, to the political developments which followed. These explain the fact that when I personally met Thatcher in London to thank her, it was as a member of Parliament and one of the leaders of the Democratic Party, now the official opposition. Helderberg had that personal and political consequence. But that is part of the story to come.

Dene Smuts was the highly reputable editor of *Fair Lady*, the leading English-language women's publication in the country. It was owned by Nasionale Pers and could therefore be expected to have a pro-government bias. But on the contrary, *Fair Lady* was edited and administered on an independent basis. Dene tells in her memoir, *Patriots and Parasites*, which was published in 2016 just before her untimely death, of a visit she made to me in London in August 1986 when I was of course still Ambassador. She describes in some detail the atmosphere on that occasion in 'the plush, panelled office with its portraits of the Foreign Minister and unique South African art pieces' and explains that I 'had done so well in this position that [I] had acquired a high media profile in both the United Kingdom and in South Africa. Because of this, we had featured him in *Fair Lady* in 1985.'

The 1986 visit, she says, was 'a curiosity visit' as her representative in London had described my performance and interrogation by mostly hostile journalists on a TV programme as 'a minor triumph'. Dene wrote that I was 'a top man prepared to declare his opposition to apartheid and admit that there were certain practices in South Africa quite indefensible in the fourth quarter of the 20th century'.

Now in 1987, when she came to see me in Helderberg, Dene described feature journalism 'as being sympathetic to the subjects, but it should not be sycophantic, and mine [as she says] never was. It must ask the difficult questions and report the answers.' Now, as she puts it, 'in the noisy, staff-packed room on Somerset West's Main Road, his only privacy Western saloon-style, pine swing doors', she pressed me for answers in a way that no other journalist had done. And I responded more fully to her than to any other journalist. Aside from respecting and liking Dene, I felt that she was completely honest with me and I gave her as much as I could. In any event, she concludes in *Patriots and Parasites*: 'The interview left me convinced that he was sincere and acting out of a sense of duty, which is what I titled the resulting feature.' It was this interview, whose publication was suppressed by Ton Vosloo of Nasionale Pers, which led to Dene's instant resignation on the grounds of editorial independence. However, the next day she learnt that Vosloo had not accepted the resignation. What followed, which Dene describes as her battle, is best read in her memoir. But one important result of this public fight, as Dene describes it, was that it had 'the eventuality of making the editorial and publishing autonomy to which Naspers paid lip service, a reality' – something which happened under the auspices of Ton Vosloo and which should be chalked up as a victory for Dene Smuts.

Dene and I reconnected in public life in the 1989 general election in the Democratic Party of which I was then one of the leaders – and whose creation I naturally trace back to the Helderberg election. Incidentally, just before her death, Dene gave me the original manuscript of the article which she had typed up of our interview and which was never published. I cherish it.

Political campaigns need funding, and in most elections this comes from the political parties. I was running this campaign as an independent and therefore without party political funding, little by way of personal finances behind me, and yet very conscious that in the final analysis I personally would be responsible for paying the bills. I would never have managed without the support of David Gant. David was involved with the Elgin Young

Farmers Association and he introduced me to this group at a late afternoon meeting. He himself offered to contribute R10,000 and challenged them also to contribute. Among the families who joined him were the Moodies, Rawbone Viljoens, Kilpins, Ben Williamses, the Simpsons, the Greens, the Downes and many others who made useful contributions. The fruit industry was subject to severe international sanctions, and as Ambassador to the UK I had done as much as I could and, as Dave says, 'pleaded our case with passion and skill'. Margaret Thatcher, aided and abetted by Lord Vestey, had opted for 'freedom of choice' for UK consumers and withstood enormous pressure from trade unions, her own countrymen and people all over the world to apply sanctions against South Africa. David felt they owed me something for my stance in this regard. In addition to those who actually made financial contributions were others who made available their homes and farms for fundraising activities.

The Helderberg election undoubtedly had enormous implications, which we shall explore. But when the counting and pontificating were over, I was presented with a number of bills that needed to be paid before the campaign could be wound up. With Dave, who clearly had played a significant role in the campaign, we decided to approach a prominent German businessman, Hans Schreiber, whom we knew to be sympathetic to our cause and who had a farm in the constituency. As he was one of our last hopes of winding up the campaign financially, it was with some anxiety that we approached him. He invited us to meet with him in the late afternoon outside his wine cellar where he proudly produced a bottle of new wine, the merits of which Dave persisted in discussing appreciatively with him at undue length – seemingly oblivious of why we were there. Probably recognising our nervousness, Hans suddenly said: 'Gentlemen, what can I do for you?' We began to explain when he laughingly interrupted us: 'But, gentlemen, that's not a problem. In Germany, we pay for our politics. How much do you need? And can I put it down to advertising?' The rest of the evening went dazzlingly.

Much has been written about the Helderberg election, but by way of general comment there are two accounts which particularly capture something of the drama of the last hours of the campaign. Jannie Momberg is responsible for the one and the other is an excellent essay by Advocate Jan Heunis, Chris Heunis's eldest son, in a book called *The Inner Circle*. Momberg describes the moment when the vote-counting was over and the result made known to the candidates. 'There was a deathly hush in the hall. Heunis was as white

as a sheet. I remember Wouter Kritzinger, his main organiser, writing down the votes and saying to Heunis: "God, meneer, dit is net 39 stemme!" (God, sir, it is only 39 votes!) Heunis, who had lost his voice, exclaimed hoarsely: "It can't be, it must be 139!" "No, sir," replied Kritzinger, "it is only 39."

'At that point Heunis turned to Denis and asked: "Are you calling for a recount?" Denis asked me what we should do. My gut feeling was to go for a recount but it was already past 3 o'clock in the morning and outside we could hear the noise of the impatient crowd. Also I had attended many counting sessions and knew how it was done.

'Two senior magistrates were in charge of the counting, and throughout the day I could see they had built an automatic recount into the system. In the light of all this, I advised Denis that we should accept the result. Over the years I have often wondered whether I took the right decision … The fact is that Denis, standing against the NP "architect of change" brought his own special message of hope and change, to which the voters responded magnificently. For the first time, people who had voted for the Nats all their lives were prepared to jump the other way, and White politics would never be the same again.'

In his account of this moment, Jan Heunis writes that his father's slim victory should have been regarded as a triumph and not a disaster given the 'formidable campaign' that we had waged. 'My father's dismay at the outcome was evident in the television broadcast of the event, for which he should have been grateful. Instead of being exuberant, he was dejected. Properly handled, his victory should have been depicted as a major one – because that is what it was. He had won against all the odds.'

Something I need to say is that there was never anything personal in my campaign against Chris Heunis. Heunis had promoted my appointment to the President's Council and, more importantly, my appointment as chairman of the Constitutional Committee. And although most reporters held Heunis responsible for packing me off to Australia, I learnt that it was Vice-President Alwyn Schlebusch, egged on by Dr Willie van Niekerk, a leading Broeder. By profession Dr Van Niekerk was a gynaecologist and apparently very popular. One day I got into a lift in which he was already standing and, as I did so, I pressed my forefinger gently into his greatly expanded midriff and in my best gynaeny voice said: 'Ah, we are doing well, aren't we?' Needless to say he chose not to attend the farewell dinner given to Anita and me by all our other colleagues before we headed for Australia.

29

HELDERBERG TO THE DEMOCRATIC PARTY

I told Anita just after balloting closed that it seemed the result would be very close; that we had come so far to end up so near (39 votes out of 18,000 cast). But it turned out that the election had a dynamic in our favour which quickly became evident.

The May 1987 election was full of surprises and a lot of disappointments. The National Party, while gaining a majority of 52% of the total vote, saw a swing of 10% away from it mainly to the Conservative Party, which gained 26% of the vote with a 13% positive swing, so replacing the Progressive Federal Party as the official parliamentary opposition. This is what prompted Archbishop Desmond Tutu to say that South Africa had entered dangerous political territory. The PFP gained 14% of the vote with 19 seats and a swing against it of 7%. As Colin Eglin writes in his memoir *Crossing the Borders of Power*, 'The election results were an immense disappointment to us.'

The New Republic Party was all but wiped out with 2% of the votes, one seat and a swing against it of 7%. And then there was the Independent Movement, as it was called, whose three candidates (Wynand Malan, Esther Lategan and I) gained just over 2% of the vote, with Malan recapturing Randburg. Van Zyl Slabbert, former leader of the PFP and a commentator during the election, described the Independents' performance 'as the most encouraging aspect of the election'. In the coming days and weeks these were realities which preoccupied my colleagues and me. There were clearly two fundamental consequences which needed to be taken into account. The first was a definite stirring among Afrikaner *verligte* voters, professionals and academics, which reflected unhappiness with the National Party and

strong interest in the Independents. Clearly, all three of the Independent candidates in the election benefited from this development.

The other major consequence of the election was an unhappiness that ran deep within the PFP and especially with Colin Eglin's leadership, and even the election campaign the party had run. The PFP went into the election with 26 sitting members of Parliament and fielded a further 26 candidates in 'winnable' seats. In other words, a total of 52 constituencies. It won 19. Of the party's campaign strategy, Dr Jan Hofmeyr, the PFP's research consultant, noted in an interview with Timothy Hughes: 'The PFP didn't get the message across because they did not have the communicators, they did not have the people they could put onto platforms and who could put the message across with credibility. Take the ad campaign of the Independents. All the images and rhetoric were well worked out. It comes across as viby, you could trust them, they've got stature, and the PFP's one was dead.'

The PFP election strategy proved fundamentally flawed at a number of other levels. But the leadership issue was critical. Eglin himself was of the view that it would be inappropriate for him to lead the party into the next election; and without knowing whether or not I was even interested in the leadership of the PFP, Colin told Hughes in an interview that he was not ready to hand over the reins to somebody like me. 'I wasn't going to rush into deals with Denis and so I had numerous guys saying, "Doing a deal with Denis can get back our seats at the next election." I agreed that the composition of the Party might have to change to accommodate Denis and Wynand but I was not, as an Old Time Prog (put it that way) for the sake of convenience, going to do a quick fix with Denis or anyone else. But, yes, there was a growing impatience to do a deal.'

As Colin admits, he was responding to pressure, and that came mainly from the Young Turks in the Southern Transvaal and party representatives in the Western Province. Very shortly after the election Robin Carlisle and Tony Leon visited me in my home in Fernwood and begged me to make myself available for the leadership of the PFP.

The fact is, as Tim Hughes puts it, 'with a third of the PFP's MPs losing their seats, eyes were furtively cast to the newly emergent "great white hopes" in the form of Wynand Malan and Denis Worrall in particular. Prominent MPs within the PFP, together with other senior members in the party, began working unilaterally on a strategy to bring Worrall's group closer to the PFP and to tap into the popularity and charisma of Worrall himself.' The leading

proponent of this strategy was Robin Carlisle, who told Hughes: 'It was very clear to us that if we were going to form a United Front there had to be some appearance or semblance of energy and direction toward Worrall's lot, because if you'd walked the streets you'd know that Malan had some marginal importance but Worrall was a very important political property. Worrall in my [Carlisle's] constituency was worth a thousand of the votes I got in the 1989 election, if not more. I told Worrall when we saw him that I thought he was good for six seats. In the end I think he was good for twelve.'

Obviously, while this was encouraging and naturally pleasing, it was not where I wanted to go. Before I left London my intention was to create a national movement by running an independent campaign not unlike that of France's Emmanuel Macron in 2017. It was to be a unique campaign. Aside from Anita, the only person I discussed this with was Barbara Bester. That was the original intention. But I was stymied when Tertius Myburgh of the *Sunday Times* brought me together on the second day of my return to South Africa with Wynand Malan and his supporters. We would both contest the May general election on an individual and independent basis, with Esther Lategan joining us a little later. But it was somewhat unreal. Although in March, the three of us adopted a manifesto, it was very much a compromise document reflecting our different approaches. There was no agreement or even understanding on policies between Wynand and me, and when I said *totsiens* to Wynand that Sunday, we were not to speak to each other again until after the election on 6 May. He didn't invite me to speak in Randburg and I didn't invite him to speak in Helderberg.

What greatly contributed to the public impression of the Independents as a political entity was the advertising campaign which we ran from Helderberg. This included, aside from advertisements in the local Cape newspapers promoting Helderberg, several centre-page spreads in the two official language newspapers with the largest national circulations, *Rapport* and the *Sunday Times*. These included photos of the three candidates and, together with headlines that talked about the need for change in bold letters, the ads had power and impact.

The advertising campaign was conceived and run – and I have to say conceived and run brilliantly – by Chris Reader, himself an advertising executive. Graham de Villiers, founder of a major advertising company and a good friend of mine, had contacted Chris quite independently of me in early 1987 and told him that I was resigning and heading home to take on the National

Party in a Cape constituency in the general election. De Villiers asked Chris, who was Cape-based, whether he would handle an advertising campaign for me. The funding would come from the private sector through Bill Yeowart, who had set up a trust for this purpose.

But as Chris puts: 'Little did I realise at the time that the Independent Movement was more of a media event rather than a political reality as Denis, Wynand and Esther never once appeared on the same platform before the election. All of the advertisements that appeared in national newspapers contained a coupon giving people four or five ways to register their support. These coupons kept arriving after the election. Seen as a market research exercise, the information they provided showed widespread interest in the Independent Movement.'

Shortly after the election I was invited to the US by a company with interests in South Africa which I advised. While in New York I also met with senior executives of the Carnegie Foundation, who, incidentally, as a follow-up early in 1988 published an article by me in the Foundation's influential journal *Ethics and International Affairs*. The title of the article was 'The Real Struggle in South Africa: An Insider's View'. And it ended with this message: 'We have made serious mistakes in our handling of the transition from an apartheid to a non-apartheid society, and certainly the present leadership is lamentably lacking in vision. But whatever our failings may be, it would be most unfortunate were outsiders, particularly in the West, to trivialise what is a very important issue for that reason. South Africa's significance (I believe) transcends apartheid. South Africa is important because, given the country's unique make-up, if we can find answers as to how our different communities can live together in peace and harmony, then nobody in the world with similar problems has reason to throw up their hands and say: "We cannot find the answer!" I think, rather significantly, I was billed "as the former South African Ambassador to the Court of St James and the founding member and leader of the anti-apartheid Independent Movement". The movement, formed during the 1987 elections in South Africa, is dedicated to achieving open-ended negotiations aimed at creating a peaceful South Africa with equal rights for all.'

But while in New York Anita phoned to tell me she had received a call from a woman in Stellenbosch who chose not to give her name but who told Anita she was deeply concerned at what 'they were doing to your husband'. I told Anita that I would deal with whatever the problem was on my

return, and within hours of my return to Cape Town Advocate De Villiers phoned me. He wanted to talk to me urgently. As I recall, it was a Sunday morning and we met at his house. He told me in rather embarrassed tones that Wynand and Esther and company wanted to do things on their own and would prefer me to stand aside.

Chris Reader worked out of an office which had to be vacated at the end of May 1987. As the coupons continued to arrive after the election and needed to be processed, he rented two small rooms in a complex on the corner of Loop and Pepper streets and hired two women to do the work. As he says: 'At the time I had visions of the office becoming the official Independent Movement's centre. However, when I arrived one morning I found a new lock blocking entry. I hadn't a clue who might have done this or why. When I contacted Denis he asked me to come immediately to Advocate Gerrit van Schalkwyk's rooms at Huguenot Chambers, where I was informed that the lock had been inserted by somebody in the NDM.'

Dave Gant refers to this episode in a private memo describing an Independent Movement public meeting held in Somerset West Town Hall the following week. As he puts it: 'For reasons of their own, Malan and Esther Lategan decided to publicly sever their connections with Worrall in a post-1987 election meeting in the Somerset West Town Hall and do their own thing. They formed the National Democratic Movement (NDM). Gill and I were on the stage and, like many Worrallites in the audience, were shocked to the core. The message to Worrall was – "Thank you for what you've done, but we will carry the torch from here on".'

Dave believes what he describes as 'the jettisoning' of me was an unfair betrayal and, as he puts it, he had no hesitation together with Jannie Momberg in emphatically responding to my telephone question to them the next morning: What do we do now? We start our own party, was their answer. And so we did.

With the spirited and ever loyal Helderberg support base forming the operating engine of the emergent party, the three of us and Keith Gurney, who was to become the Independent Party's secretary-general, began promoting the IP all over the country. As a result the Independent Movement met in Somerset West on 17 March 1988 to form the Independent Party with Dave and Jannie as co-chairpersons, Keith Gurney as secretary-general, and me as leader. In August 1988 the IP held its first congress in Stellenbosch. The congress reiterated the IP's past commitment to a non-racial, democratic

and free-market South Africa, and also committed the party to the introduction of a proportional representation electoral system and a Bill of Rights.

Jannie Momberg makes an interesting point in his book. As a result of the
NDM taking in prominent PFP members with close ties to the ANC, the reality was that it had moved so far left that it had become difficult for Afrikaans-
speaking voters to support it – whereas the Independent Movement had not
changed its position since the election, remaining to the left of the National
Party, rather than the left of the PFP. And this was reflected in the respective
support for the IP and the NDM in polls conducted toward the end of 1988.

In the Cape and Natal, where the IP was particularly active, it was the
biggest opposition party in both provinces with 21% in Natal and 18% in the
Cape, compared with the NDM's 3.5% in Natal and 3.5% in the Cape. As
a matter of interest, the PFP stood at 14.6% in Natal and 8.6% in the Cape.
Tim Hughes in his dissertation observes that the Independent Party achieved
this position of popular support without the help of the NDM. And in the
next stage of political party development, the NDM's participation, if not
survival, was on the Independent Party's coat-tails.

Wynand and I had been parliamentarians together before my appointment to the diplomatic corps. We were friends but not particularly close.
And as I have indicated, I don't think either of us particularly welcomed
Tertius Myburgh, editor of the *Sunday Times*, bringing us together on that
second day after my return to South Africa. As a matter of fact Wynand, a
couple of months later, told the country that linking up with Denis Worrall
was the biggest mistake he had made. And so it was that we had nothing to
do with each other in the run-up to the election, although Chris Reader, our
publicist, linked us prominently in the centre-fold advertisements he placed
in *Rapport* and the *Sunday Times*.

But it seems that when we got together to plan the promotion of the
Independent Movement, difficulties immediately arose. Jannie Momberg
and Dave Gant have both written about this, speculating what the reasons
were. I remember several occasions when Wynand and I talked but failed to
come to a satisfactory conclusion. I think the main reason was that we had a
different approach to politics and neither of us really wanted to subordinate
himself to the other. Regarding potential differences between us, the main
one was the suggestion that Wynand was more persuaded than I that the
ANC was an indispensable player in any proposed answer to our situation.
But that is not correct.

When Donald Woods told me as the Ambassador in London that the ANC wanted me to meet with its president, Oliver Tambo, for that very reason I took the invitation extremely seriously. And, quite frankly, had it not been that I was in resignation mode and heading back to stand in an election, I would have consented. But imagine what PW Botha would have done in that Ermelo speech if he could have cast me as the ANC's rather than the British industries' secret candidate in the election? I could have kissed goodbye to Helderberg and any of the political benefits it apparently brought.

Jannie tells of a meeting in Somerset West in late October 1987, attended by Advocate De Villiers, Wynand, Dave Gant, me and Jannie (who chaired it), which decided that there was no possibility of a reconciliation between the two groups. This resulted in each taking a different route. Wynand formed the National Democratic Movement, taking with him Pierre Cronje, Pieter Schoeman and Peter Gastrow of the PFP, as well as Advocate De Villiers and Esther Lategan. They didn't form a political party, but stayed as a loose movement. Jannie writes: 'Those of us who had been part of the Worrall campaign in Helderberg worked very hard to move to a point where we could form a political party around the ideals of the Independents.' Wynand would rejoin us, but it would be as a result of the Independent Party demonstrating real potential at the polls. So much for differences.

I would like to end this chapter on a positive note by expressing a personal opinion in respect of Wynand's approach to politics. When Wynand spoke of the necessity of establishing relations with extra-parliamentary movements, and the ANC in particular, he meant this with an intensity of feeling I don't believe any other leading white politician experienced. Most of us – including the PFP, academics, and editorial writers – when speaking or writing of the importance of relating to the ANC, spoke or wrote of it as being in Lusaka or wherever, but across the border. It was over there, in the distance. It was almost an international relations problem. Foreign Minister Pik Botha, when speaking against me in the Strand (in the Helderberg constituency), said: 'The ANC is coming! Beware! Pasop! Vote Heunis!' For Wynand, on the other hand, 'The ANC is in your kitchen, the ANC's looking after your baby, the ANC is the guy who puts petrol in your car.' Remember, we are talking of South Africa in the 1980s. Wynand's approach was a real-time one. And I greatly respected him for it.

ESTABLISHMENT OF THE
DEMOCRATIC PARTY

I believe the period immediately after the general election of 6 May
1987 and into the second half of 1988 was critical for parliamentary
opposition in the country. This was also a time when the PFP and the
Independent Party started discovering each other. As regards the association
with Wynand Malan, my associates and I were not unhappy when he formed
the NDM and went off on his own. There were very real differences between
us in style, strategy and end-result, and, quite frankly as several market surveys conclusively showed, we had much more pulling power than the NDM.

As regards the PFP, the major opposition party to the left of the National
Party, I similarly communicated my wish for independence to Colin Eglin
when I was still in London; and when back in Cape Town I declined with
thanks his offer of the safe seat of Groote Schuur in the coming election.
There would come a time when close relations with the PFP would be in our
interest, but my colleagues and I had first to establish ourselves to our own
satisfaction, at which point we expected the PFP would really need us. In
fact, we were adamant that we would, as a matter of strategy and in the early
stages of the development of the Independent Party, privately and publicly
emphasise our intention not to be submerged in the PFP – something which
Dave Gant was particularly effective in getting across.

The 1987 election was a disaster for the PFP. Ideologically it had lost
focus, organisationally and at the level of personnel it had been badly dam-
aged, and in terms of positioning and popular support it had been acutely
undermined. Much of this malaise could be traced back to Van Zyl Slabbert's
resignation as leader, and his and Alex Boraine's establishment of IDASA

and the downplaying of Parliament in favour of developing relations with extra-parliamentary players. But whatever the reasons, Tim Hughes's view is that by 1987 the PFP was in the throes of a deep and possibly terminal 'existential crisis'. Lawrence Schlemmer's research also showed that PFP support had declined drastically from some 20% in February 1987 to 9% in early 1988. As certain leading PFP members saw it, the question was whether the party could, by itself, reconstruct its image, its policies, its public appeal and its donor base, while neutralising the impact of the Independent Party and recapturing its lost electoral support. It seemed unlikely that this could be done in the short term and with a constitutionally required election loom-ing possibly within six months. The appropriate strategy for the achievement of these goals became the central motivation and focus of the party.

The extent of the party's crisis was clear from the internal inquisition which followed the PFP's electoral performance. It was brutal. Those MPs who had lost their seats were particularly critical. Robin Carlisle, who had developed the party's 'turbo-charged strategy' and who lost the Wynberg seat, resigned his position as secretary-general, and recommended that Colin Eglin and federal executive chairman Ken Andrew and party chairman Peter Gastrow also resign. For many in the party the failure was one of politi-cal marketing. Brian Goodall, who lost his Edenvale seat, conducted his own research and found that, had he resigned from the PFP and stood as an Independent in 1987, he would have won the seat. Tony Leon, who with Goodall was one of the leaders of the Southern Transvaal Young Turks, and who would play a leading role in getting the PFP into better shape, was also very critical of the party's marketing. He was likewise critical of Colin's leadership, instead favouring Zach de Beer. Other considerations aside, there was support for De Beer as it was thought he would regain business support, which I was believed to have generated for the IP.

In response to the party's problems, and the diversity of opinions as to what it should do, the PFP held a series of 'think tanks', and in April 1988 (one month after the launch of the Independent Party) the PFP federal executive appointed a powerful three-person commission comprising Colin Eglin, Zach de Beer and Errol Moorcroft, to seek ways 'of bringing about an understanding or unification between like-minded groups'.

Later in 1988, when he believed we ourselves were ready, Dave Gant produced a short but persuasive memo for the Independent leadership mak-ing the case for the Independent Party to explore possible relations with the

PFP. The thrust of what he proposed was based on the fact that the PFP had serious problems and there were important elements in that party who saw some of the answers in an association with us. In any event, it would not be to anybody's advantage in the opposition to the left of the government to contest the forthcoming election as independent entities, as this would split the anti-NP vote. We also knew that the PFP in 1987 had not made any sort of impact on the *verligte* Afrikaans voters that market surveys had identified, and it was unlikely to do any better – even if Zach replaced Colin – in any forthcoming election.

Dave also claimed that we (the IP) had the leadership, the winning image and potential voter appeal which the PFP was sadly lacking. He argued that, given the views and thrust of the Young Turks and other groupings within the PFP, the IP was strong enough to make a deal with the PFP while insisting on the new party incorporating the Independent Party's essential principles. He was quite adamant that we had all the aces – and that was how we went into talks with the PFP. And we did so only after extensive consultations with our members. As the main purpose of the exercise was to bring together all parliamentary groups to the left of the NP, Wynand and his NDM were invited to join.

As I've explained, my relationship with Colin Eglin and Zach de Beer went back to my early university days when Colin was leader of the United Party in the Cape Peninsula and I was leader of the party's youth and Zach was MP for Maitland. Colin and I went our separate ways but maintained a cordial relationship over the years. He was 'Mr Grumpy' to many people but not to me. But in his memoir I think the chapter he found most painful to write was the one after the 1987 election describing the negotiations between him, Wynand Malan and myself to bring together our respective parties and create what was eventually the Democratic Party. The chapter opens with the following paragraph:

'Frustrations still ran high among members of the PFP Parliamentary Caucus as the 1988 session began. As an opposition we were fragmented, displaced by Treurnicht's Conservative Party as the official opposition. Among parties generally opposed to apartheid the NRP lingered – with only one MP, it was swiftly fading. Wynand Malan's recently formed National Democratic Movement (NDM), with three MPs, was quietly establishing its relevance. Worrall's Independent Movement, although it had no MPs, was active in holding public meetings, recruiting members and attracting

considerable press attention. Worrall appeared to be gaining support among voters who, while dissatisfied with the Nationalists, were not disposed to supporting the PFP. We were also hurting from the defection of three MPs.'

An important factor of which Colin was made very aware from within the PFP was that he was held responsible to a high degree for the PFP's poor performance in the 1987 election, and there was a strong sentiment favouring a change of leadership. Complicating the situation and the potential negotiations was the fact that, while my senior colleagues and I realised that, given another general election, it was very desirable that the opposition unite, it was not something we were enthusiastic about. As Colin admits, the IP was doing well and, given its performance, we didn't think linking up with the PFP was the most beneficial course for us to take.

Similar reservations applied to Wynand's NDM. And a complicating factor was the difficult relationship between the IP and the NDM. As a result the negotiations setting up a single party united in opposition to apartheid and to the National Party promised to be very tough. And so they were.

I was conscious of two critical considerations affecting our election fighting ability. The first was that we were not in the short time of our existence as a party able to generate the membership base that was needed. This was very evident in our poor performance in local government elections. We simply would not have enough people on the ground to seriously contest a general election. And secondly, there was the question of finance. As I have explained, Harry Oppenheimer supported all the personal ventures for which I approached him down the years, and he had also supported through Gavin Relly my decision to contest Helderberg as an independent. Financing the Independent Party was something else, and yet when I saw him with my request his response was immediately positive. However, he asked whether I would mind if he discussed my request with Zach and Colin first. Of course not, and very much to the credit of the PFP leaders, the Independent Party joined the list of enlightened political parties that Mr Oppenheimer had supported down the years.

In the following months, informal discussions took place between the Eglin-De Beer-Moorcroft team and Wynand Malan and several of my colleagues and me. However, as Colin acknowledges, no progress was made in negotiating any formal cooperation agreement. Meantime, in June Colin advised senior executives that he intended standing down at the Federal Congress of the party on 3 August and he expected Zach to succeed him.

There were two factors that influenced the situation at this point and gave impetus to the unification process. The first was the so-called Forth Force, a number of prominent Afrikaans academics like Marinus Wiechers, Sampie Terreblanche and Wimpie de Klerk, elder brother of FW de Klerk; and the second, rather surprisingly, was the controversial businessman Dr Louis Luyt, whose role I will explain presently.

Wishing to move things along, Zach, Wynand and I appointed a small inter-party committee to determine whether there was common ground on issues of importance for taking the process of a realignment further. It comprised Dave Gant and Jannie Momberg from the Independent Party, Esther Lategan and Jannie Hofmeyr from the NDM, and Tiaan van der Merwe and Colin Eglin (as chairperson) for the PFP. The committee met informally on several occasions analysing what Dave Gant called the 'balance sheets' of the three groups: their assets and liabilities, cash balances, leadership qualities and supporting poll results, etc. Things progressed to the point where a more formal meeting was held in Colin Eglin's parliamentary office, but as Jannie says: 'It was soon evident that if the problems between the Worrall and Malan camps could not be resolved, nothing would come of the meeting to establish one party.' And after an hour or so of bickering between us and little prospect of progress, Colin suggested the two groups go off and separately resolve our differences before continuing the discussion. And this we did. Jannie, Wynand, Dave and I went off to the well-known Nelson's Eye Steakhouse in Hof Street. The steaks were good and the red wine flowed, and suddenly Wynand said: 'Kêrels, ons kan hierdie lot skaak!' (Chaps, we can hijack this lot.)

The result was that we didn't go back to meet with Colin in his office but chose instead to take some decisions. Wynand and I would be the leaders of the new party (not as yet named) and Zach would be chairman. Dave Gant wrote this up in a flowery report which he issued to the *Sunday Times*, which very appropriately published it on the front page. The *Sunday Times* also reported somebody purporting to speak for me who said I was ready to abandon the talks if they did not proceed on the basis we had agreed to. Colin, understandably, was furious. In fact, so furious that years later when he published his memoirs he took the time and space to excoriate Dave.

The *Sunday Times* carried the story over to the next week, when that morning I received a telephone call from Dr Louis Luyt, which went something like this: 'Dr Worrall, PW Botha is besig om ons land in sy glory te

stuur en julle gedra julself soos 'n klomp blerrie kinders!' (The President is busy sending the country to hell and you and your fellows behave like a lot of children.) He went on to say that he expected to see us at his home in Johannesburg the following Saturday.

While the name Louis Luyt will be familiar to older readers, I need to say something about him. Luyt wrote a memoir *Walking Proud* and Max du Preez wrote an excellent biography of him. Louis was born in a small town in the Karoo and was part of the Afrikaner population known as *arme blankes* (poor whites). His father was a labourer who subsequently joined the South African Railways. Until around his 16th year Louis felt despised by his school fellows, by his teachers, in fact by everyone, and as Max says: 'Other poor kids accepted their fate and lived ordinary lives. Louis Luyt spent his entire adult life avenging his first 16 years.' The significance of the age is that Louis was to be big, eventually 6 foot 4 and big-framed and a very good rugby player, which ensured respect from his fellow Afrikaners.

But Louis was also a big thinker. I first met him in the year I took off from my full-time UCT studies to write my master's dissertation. I wanted to experience something of commerce, and Caltex employed me as an executive trainee and sent me to the Bloemfontein branch for a three-month rounding-off experience, and there I met and got to know Louis. He was a dispatch clerk in a back office controlling diesel deliveries to farmers. That was his first step in creating the base for a highly successful fertiliser company, brewery and other businesses which relied on Afrikaner support, in particular farming support. His business ethics were sometimes questionable but he was uniquely self-confident and everything about him was big – from his office, his car (a long, low-slung Cadillac of that time) and his business ideas, to his plans for Transvaal and South African rugby, and what political actions he undertook or encouraged.

For example, he was thinking big when in 1988 (to PW Botha's and FW de Klerk's fury), taking with him rugby supremo Dr Danie Craven, he visited the still-banned ANC in Harare in an attempt to normalise South Africa's sporting relations. And he was thinking big when he phoned me that Sunday morning and virtually instructed me and the other two to be at his Parkwood home in Johannesburg (called Solitaire, which incidentally incorporated a squash court) where Zach, Wynand and I and our respective teams arrived as agreed, to be joined by Professor Wimpie de Klerk (representing the Fourth Force) whom Luyt had invited to chair the meeting.

With Louis more or less standing over us, the meeting went well, and the media, who were there in droves, organised by Luyt, were issued a statement afterwards to the effect that the PFP, the IP and the NDM would cease to exist and a new party (yet to be named) would be established. While there would continue to be informal discussions between the four (the party leaders and the representatives of the Fourth Force), major decision-making would be postponed to a meeting in January.

Louis Luyt must therefore be regarded as one of the founders of the Democratic Party. He continued his interest and at one point suggested to Dave Gant that, if the three of us couldn't get our act together, he was willing to lead the new party. And he was not happy when we did agree on the co-leadership concept. Nonetheless, he was an honoured guest at the launch of the Democratic Party. He was seated with the three of us and Wimpie de Klerk. He was asked to speak but declined. However, he accepted appointment to the executive of the party.

Louis describes a good part of this in his *Walking Proud*. But what he also mentions is that Zach approached him twice to support him (Zach) as the single leader, which I don't think was exactly kosher, given that the troika was based on an agreement between the three of us. Luyt says that the second time Zach approached him was at his seaside house in Ballito when Zach was staying in nearby La Lucia with Harry Oppenheimer. Louis writes that his response was: 'Zach, you are all fighting over the question of leadership. It is my view, this is something that will evolve over time. The real leader will not be picked. He will emerge.' Luyt writes: 'After he [Zach] left, I sat down and took serious stock of the situation. Over the previous few months, I had spent considerable amounts of my money and endless hours in order to form this new party. I tried to focus on the ultimate goal, namely, winning the hearts and souls of the undecided electorate and eventually ousting the Nationalists. The three leaders had, in the meanwhile been almost entirely preoccupied with the battle of who should be in charge. The time had come to bow out, I told Adri [his wife] … I wrote a letter to all three members of the Troika, resigning from the executive and wishing them well. Zach de Beer responded by letter, accusing me of never having been "one of us" – whatever that meant. Wynand Malan called me long afterwards to tell me how sorry he had been about my decision. Only Denis Worrall wrote me a very decent letter to thank me for my contribution.'

At the end of January 1989 the scheduled meeting took place in Cape

Town at the home of Aaron Searle. Clearly there were some big issues to discuss, among them the new party's name and, of course, who was to lead it. At that meeting it was informally agreed that the new party would be called the Democratic Party, and it would have three leaders – De Beer, Malan and Worrall. It was also agreed that the founding of the new party would take place in Johannesburg on Saturday, 8 April 1989. My associates and I agreed that on that preceding Friday afternoon the Independent Party would hold its dissolution conference. I spoke, as did Jannie Momberg and Dave Gant, and there were numerous expressions of both regret and hope.

However, as one would expect, there was a much stronger sense of nostalgic disappointment at the PFP's formal dissolution, also on the Friday. As Colin says, for those who had made so many sacrifices for the PFP it was a very moving experience. This was particularly so for the 'fifty-niners' such as Helen Suzman, Ray Swart, Max Borkum, Zach de Beer and Colin himself, and others who had helped found the Progressive Party thirty years before in November 1959. Colin says they all made brief farewell speeches. Not all of them welcomed the new development. Helen, whose magnificent contribution to civil liberties over more than thirty years was certainly acknowledged within IP ranks, described the IP–PFP union – rather originally, I have always thought – 'as the biggest take-over since Entebbe airport!' However, it was certainly a measure of the Independent Party's achievement that there was only one dissenting hand when the PFP dissolution vote was put to its delegates. That hand belonged to Dr Marius Barnard, brother of Chris Barnard.

Colin graphically describes the next day when some sixteen hundred people attended the inauguration and launch of the Democratic Party in the auditorium of the Johannesburg College of Education: 'For many delegates the faces they saw, the names they heard, and the people they met were new. The excitement generated by the newness was heightened by the expectations and the uncertainties of what lay ahead.' Wimpie de Klerk spelled out the new party's principles; and Zach, Wynand and I each made short speeches and were subsequently confirmed as co-leaders of the DP.

Tony Leon in the book *On the Contrary* describes the speeches as follows: 'The speeches of the three joint leaders were, appropriately, studies in contrast. Zach was worthy but a little flat; while Malan was almost semi-mystical, invoking "paradigm shifts" and "flex flows", which I thought verged on mumbo-jumbo. Worrall, however, set the Congress alight with a

brainstorming extempore performance, perhaps somewhat light in content. The excellence of his bilingual delivery electrified the crowd.'

Jannie Momberg, who chaired the meeting, tells of his first and only difficult encounter. Some months before, in a widely publicised speech he had said the IP wanted to establish an original party and 'not the PFP in drag'. When Helen Suzman arrived and he wanted to show her to her reserved seat, she told him: 'I will not, and unless you apologise for that rude speech you made in Grahamstown, I am not even going to attend this bloody conference!' Jannie writes that it took all his skill to calm her down and get her to sit in her seat. And at the opening of the conference when he welcomed the guests, he says he made a special point of welcoming Mrs Suzman and spoke glowingly of her contribution to South African politics over so many years. At tea-time she came to him and said: 'You are doing very well. Let's forget this morning's differences!'

Jannie was appointed to the executive committee of the new party, as was Dave Gant, who really was the chief negotiator for the Independent Party in the merger discussions. Dave was appointed vice-chairman of the National Board together with Tiaan van der Merwe, and Dave was later appointed chairman of the Federal Council of the Democratic Party.

Like me, I am sure many people must have wondered, given the significant role which Professor Willem (Wimpie) de Klerk, FW's older brother, played in setting up the Democratic Party, how this affected the relationship between the two of them. Wimpie discusses this in his book *FW de Klerk: A Man in His Time.* 'My own role in the founding of the Democratic Party – as chairman of the talks and the merger and as a candidate for the party's leadership – was deeply disturbing to FW. We had some heated words, followed by penetrating critical discussions on the political policies of the National Party and the Democratic Party. Throughout these discussions – from November 1988 to September 1989 – FW maintained that he found the Democratic Party's policy unacceptable. He had strong reservations especially on the party's attitude to the entrenchment of group rights (which he then still saw as the rights of racial groups). Nevertheless, I got the impression that he was showing a new sensitivity to the fact that the National Party's policy had reached a dead-end and that the Democratic Party was offering a clearcut policy option with distinct possibilities. The road he has followed, step-by-step, since 1986 has gone in this direction.'

31

THE GENERAL ELECTION OF 6 SEPTEMBER 1989

In varying degrees increasing voter support was the driving force behind the merger of the three political parties and the creation of the Democratic Party. The National Democratic Movement (NDM), particularly given Wynand Malan's attitude towards Parliament and commitment to the extra-parliamentary Mass Democratic Movement, was less interested in expanding its parliamentary base. My senior colleagues and I in the Independent Party were happy with our growth prospects, particularly as market surveys showed we were drawing *verligte* Afrikaans support away from the National Party as well as PFP supporters. In fact, we were the biggest opposition party to the left of the National Party. But there obviously were two strategic considerations – finance and membership on the ground – which encouraged us, particularly with a general election around the corner, to respond positively to the overtures from the PFP, which at that time, quite frankly, desperately needed to recast itself. As Tim Hughes wrote: 'It was clear from the performance and public response to the Independents [in 1987] that a spirit of renewal was gripping important elements of white moderate politics, which was in turn beginning to lay the groundwork for the sea change in the 1989 general election. The Independents had demonstrated that there existed a potential dynamic among large sections of the white community for reform, but that the packaging, marketing style, identity and rhetoric of the PFP was the wrong political vessel in which to carry that message.'

The coming general election would clearly be the test of the unification strategy we had followed. The three parties had merged their identities and

formed a single party but under three co-leaders. The question this naturally raised was which of the leaders available would most effectively expand the new party's membership. In terms of the guidelines the party had set out for itself, the leader would need to appeal both to disaffected National Party supporters (the so-called 22%), while engaging the extra-parliamentary leadership of the Mass Democratic Movement. Accordingly, as one commentator put it, the party required a leader with a 'broad South Africanism'. The person I myself would have said came closest to this brief was Frederik van Zyl Slabbert. But aside from the fact that he had precluded himself by his own reservations about rejoining a parliamentary political party, and while he would be very acceptable to Wynand, the fact is that he was unacceptable to many within the PFP because of his past political inconsistencies.

These considerations aside, I think he lacked political staying power and, quite frankly, while it may seem a strange thing to say, he was politically naïve, as was evident from his bizarre proposal to Colin Eglin in January 1986 just before his sudden resignation as leader of the PFP and therefore as official Leader of the Opposition. His proposal was that all PFP MPs resign from Parliament and then contest their seats again – on the basis that those re-elected would not take their seats until the government repealed the Population Registration Act. After being told this, Colin writes: 'I was filled with despair at what Slabbert intended – and disbelief that a person as adept as he was, could have produced such a flawed and fanciful scheme.'

In respect to his sudden resignation as party leader the *Sunday Times* editorially commented: 'Most of all, Dr Slabbert will be remembered as a captain who at the height of the most serious storm his country has known laid his own secret plans and simply helicopered off the ship leaving officers and crew in the lurch.' This he did to the disappointment and anger of people like Tony Leon, who was in the middle of a local government campaign.

Another blow to the PFP was Alex Boraine's resignation. He was PFP member of Parliament for Pinelands who resigned with Slabbert and joined him in establishing IDASA, an organisation which played a major role in bringing together influential South Africans and leaders of the still-outlawed ANC. A prominent example of this was the 1987 Dakar Conference. Boraine, incidentally, was later appointed by President Mandela to co-chair with Archbishop Desmond Tutu the Truth and Reconciliation Commission from 1996 to 1998.

With Slabbert out of the way, attention focused on the three co-leaders.

Tim Hughes makes the very valid point that 'the leadership issue was more than just a question of personality and power. Negotiators and their allies would be set a clear dilemma: the choice of leader would cast the mould for the identity and policy thrust of the party, and no single leader was acceptable to the other two, or to the disparate constituencies and formations to which they respectively made an appeal.' Hughes goes on to say this was demonstrated by a series of polls among white voters which indicated that 'Worrall enjoyed more support amongst National Party supporters (the 22%) than the other two leaders. Worrall had also shown up well in the Indaba and *Argus* polls in 1988. A survey of National Party supporters by Mark en Mening indicated that the IP had made considerable inroads among National Party supporters. Of a representative sample, 33% said that they would vote for another party if the NP did not put up a candidate in their constituency. Of these 4% would have voted for the PFP, 5% for the NDM, 8% for the CP and 16% for the IP. The survey of NP voters indicated that support for Worrall to be elected leader of the new party stood at 32%, Malan 20%, Slabbert 13% and De Beer a mere 3%. The results clearly indicate that, were the new party to have based its policy and appeal on expanding its support base amongst disaffected NP supporters, this would best be achieved under Worrall's leadership.'

For the record, I was quite content being a co-leader and subsequently a member of the troika. But if it did come to having a single leader I would have backed Tiaan van der Merwe, PFP member of Parliament for Green Point and one of the most intelligent, politically committed people I have known, with the personality and nature to go with it. He would have satisfied Wynand, most PFP members and certainly my associates. Sadly, he died long before his time in 1991 in a senseless car accident.

The Democratic Party announced after a meeting in Cape Town in the first weekend of February 1989 that, although it would take a couple of months for the party to be up and running, we regarded the new party as an 'accomplished fact' as from that time. We announced a steering committee of the DP which would supervise the transfer of the membership of the three political formations to that of the DP.

After the announcement of the intention to form a new party I held a press conference to the effect: 'The Democratic Party will combine the Independent Party's ability to cut into the NP power base; the PFP's organisational strength; and the NDM's extra-Parliamentary credibility. At the

moment DP support is about 24% of the electorate and some believe it could be as much as 30%. The issue of leadership was a political necessity, given the need to consolidate our support. To have elected one person would have been a mistake. Each of us has our different strengths and combined we make a formidable team. It enables us to give full expression to our individual talents. Our commitment is to the establishment of a new political party with a personality which is distinctive from the PFP, the IP and the NDM. Toward this end our immediate objectives are: the consolidation of existing memberships; the recruitment of those many South Africans who share our values and are looking for a new political home; and the achievement of supporting credibility across the political spectrum.' I argued that it was a mistake to see the joint leadership as an interim arrangement, as it had come about as a result of discussions between us and from a commitment to alliance politics.

For the Democratic Party the September 1989 general elections were a baptism of fire. The National Party had existed for 77 years, for 41 of which it had governed the country. On election day, 6 September, the DP would have existed for 150 days. But in my opinion the calling of the election had the effect of galvanising the party. I told the *Cape Times* of 7 April 1989 after the announcement of the election: 'It means in effect that after only two years there is a chance of winning back the seats the PFP lost in 1987 and getting a creative party as the official opposition.' And in a statement to *The Citizen*, in which I sought to bring the business community squarely behind the DP, I spoke of 'a buoyancy' in the DP and our supporters: 'There is a buoyancy, a sense of mission, and a sense of purpose in the DP. And all of this, I would like the business community of South Africa to know, is being done on a shoestring compared to the almost endless cash resources which seem to be available to the National Party. I suggest businessmen who talk about "giving FW a chance" think again. They are backing the wrong horse.'

My co-leader Zach de Beer stamped a clear liberal-democratic identity on the new party when he summarised the DP philosophy as having two overriding objectives: firstly, the creation of a single harmonious nation; and, secondly, to provide all with a steadily improving quality of life. For Zach the basis of harmonious nation-building was the principle of universal justice. This meant that citizens had to enjoy all of the fundamental human rights characteristic of Western democracies. And I ensured the party was strongly committed to a federalist constitutional approach.

Opposition parties to the left of the National Party have always had difficulty in responding to charges of 'one person one vote' and the 'common society'. The DP manifesto responded to this by stating: 'Our opponents often claim that DP stands for one man one vote in a unitary system. This is not true. We stand for universal adult franchise in the federal system. South Africa should consist of federal states that will conduct their affairs in whichever way they choose, provided this does not conflict with the constitution or bill of rights.' The manifesto document recommended that the powers of national government be limited to matters of national concern such as foreign affairs and national finance.

At a national board meeting on 31 May 1989 it was decided the party should fight the election on a 'broad' basis. Apart from the 19 seats the DP already held, it would focus on a further 24 'winnable' constituencies. These comprised 10 in the Cape, 7 in Natal and 7 in the Transvaal. The board decided to expand its support base by contesting a further 29 seats and another 16 which were categorised as 'flag wave' seats. These were seats in which the party didn't have a ghost of a chance but where groundwork for the future would be laid.

On the Reef a win for Brian Goodall, a very good and old friend – when I was at Wits I supervised his honours degree – in Edenvale and a win in Hillbrow and a good performance in Bezuidenhout were expected. We also expected to do well in Natal where the IP had campaigned very actively for the incorporation of the New Republic Party (NRP), the successor to the United Party, and as many of its members as possible.

As a consequence, the IP had been the biggest party to the left of the National Party in that province. I was also standing in Berea, Durban. Incidentally, Berea didn't fall into my lap – I had to fight a nomination contest for it without any support from Ray Swart, the PFP retiring member. I was never able to establish what the margin of my win was, but all I know is that it was very close. As regards the election itself, I won it with a majority of 4,279. I was to be the member of Parliament for Berea until just before the 1994 general election when I resigned.

In the Cape Robin Carlisle was expected to regain Wynberg, my old friend Jannie Momberg was looking good in Simonstown, and Dave Gant could be expected to put up a tough fight in Helderberg. In the Eastern Cape and the Border, DP hopes were pinned on Albany and Walmer, both of which the PFP had lost to the NP in 1997, and King Williamstown was an outside possibility.

We articulated our immediate electoral goal as one of forcing a hung parliament. This would be achieved by winning over on a national basis those *verligte* Afrikaans voters who had supported me in Helderberg and who we knew from market surveys were out there; and through strategically placed candidates in constituencies we knew we couldn't win, who would draw sufficient NP votes to allow the Conservative Party (CP) to win the constituency. By winning the targeted 43 seats, together with the effect of splitting the reform vote, the National Party's representation in Parliament would be reduced to less than the 84 seats required to form a government. There is no doubt that this strategy had the effect of unnerving the National Party. We received back-door approaches from high-level members of the National Party asking us not to put up candidates in certain constituencies where the hung parliament strategy was likely to work. But we made it clear that 'We would not be party to any quiet deals to frustrate the democratic choice of voters'. And in respect of one particular proposal, I told the *Cape Times* that it was clear that 'the DP was already shaking the NP tree', which irked F.W. de Klerk into saying: 'One would think Denis Worrall is running for president!' By the way, it was pleasing that the *Financial Mail* editorially supported our hung parliament strategy.

Hennie Bester, then a very prominent Stellenbosch student leader, was the DP's candidate in Stellenbosch and expressed this positive sentiment. He said his information was that 70% of the student body supported the DP and its policies. He made the point that a majority of Afrikaans speakers could be the most committed advocates for change if their sense of justice were acti-vated. He added: 'The crucial difference in this election is that for the first time in decades we have an opposition party to the left of the government acceptable to Afrikaans South Africans.' Importantly, too, the DP had been requested to put up candidates in traditional NP and even CP heartlands. Both Peter Soal and I were flown by DP supporters to Klerksdorp. I was also invited to a black tie affair in Boksburg and a tea in Springs.

An important difference in my view between the Democratic Party and the PFP was one of degree rather than principle: it was a case of different strategic and tactical emphases. The DP was distinguished from the PFP in that it was imbued with a sense of the importance of the acquisition of power. I believe that the DP had taken to heart the hard political lesson that a political party, no matter how morally righteous, cannot stray too far ahead of its electorate, particularly during the time of an election.

In July the DP received an important electoral boost from an unexpected source when the IDASA executive director and former PFP chairman, Dr Alex Boraine, endorsed the party. Boraine's endorsement was an important statement as it lent credibility to participation in the House of Assembly election and gave credence to the potential for cooperative alliance strategies between progressive white-system politicians and the extra-parliamentary movement.

As Boraine had left Parliament in 1986 shortly after Slabbert on the 'irrelevance of Parliament' ticket, this was an important shift. Reinforcing this was the qualified support given to the DP by twelve left-wing white organisations a month before the election. The Five Freedoms Forum made a statement encouraging their members to support the white progressive candidates in their constituency, particularly if they had an interest in the extra-parliamentary movement.

While things were looking up for the Democratic Party, the National Party was experiencing serious problems. In contrast to the crisp and focused DP election manifesto, the National Party's five-year plan was riddled with contradictions. The degree of disillusionment within the NP was also illustrated by the lukewarm reception elements of its traditionally supportive media gave its manifesto. These included *Beeld* and *Rapport*. A further indicator of the NP decline was that in contrast to the pulling power of the DP's leadership ticket, the NP's past traditional drawcards failed to ignite the public's imagination in the run-up to the election. During the campaign Defence Minister Magnus Malan drew a 'crowd' of 38 at a meeting at Voortrekkerhoogte, while later attracting 80 in Uvongo and the same number at the Strand. Deputy Minister of Transport and Durbanville MP Frik van Deventer managed a total of 17 at one of his constituency meetings. Ron Miller and Sakkie Pretorius raised 30 at a Gardens meeting. Minister of Finance Barend du Plessis drew 180 at a Welgemoed meeting, while on the same night the DP's 26-year-old Stellenbosch candidate, Hennie Bester, attracted more than 700. When Du Plessis spoke at Stellenbosch after Bester, only 400 attended. In Welgemoed Wynand Malan drew 400 supporters, more than twice Du Plessis's attendance. And I'm happy to say in my final meetings I attracted 1,200 and 1,500 supporters respectively, compared to the 700 De Klerk drew in his final campaign meeting.

Entering the final month of the long 1989 election campaign, the NP was a more embattled party than it had ever been in its 41 years of governance.

And a critical turning point in the election was the resignation of President P.W. Botha three weeks before election day.

De Klerk moved quickly to consolidate his hold on power. He embarked on an intense campaign to recapture the considerable amount of ground lost by the NP in previous months. De Klerk abandoned any hope of recapturing the white right-wing and henceforth sought to contest the moderate, reformist 'middle ground' by campaigning on the theme of 'negotiation for a new constitution'. Tim Hughes comments on all this by saying that to a degree De Klerk recaptured undecided and drifting support by bringing a new image and hope to disillusioned NP supporters. This image was buttressed by successful trips to Britain, Europe and Africa where he had been well received. For many National Party supporters De Klerk projected sincerity of purpose and reason, which had all but been destroyed under P.W. Botha. And I have to say I agree with this sentiment.

In the last month of the campaign the Democratic Party experienced two problems – firstly, we had 'peaked' too soon; and secondly, Archbishop Desmond Tutu challenged fellow Anglicans to consider whether they could in all conscience vote in an election whilst their fellow black Anglicans were excluded. Frank Chikane of the South African Council of Churches similarly called on people not to vote in the elections. Zach de Beer responded to the call for an election boycott, saying it was regrettable and that it would cost the DP a few seats.

The concluding statements of the NP and the DP reveal an interesting contrast. F.W. de Klerk on the eve of the election acknowledged: 'We've almost reached the end of one of the longest election campaigns in South Africa's history. Never again will we do it.'

It was left to me to wind up our campaign and I did so 'by asking White South Africans to send a message to the international community – to bankers, to stockbrokers, to multinational corporations and to fellow black South Africans – the days of apartheid are over.' The election results showed that they were.

The accompanying table summarises the results of the 1989 election with comparative figures for the 1987 election.

After a long and difficult campaign the Democratic Party, which was born out of Helderberg, demonstrated unprecedented support in the country for a politically all-inclusive system of government. The DP came into the election with 19 seats in the House of Assembly. At the end of the election it

held 33 seats, drawing 10% of the white vote away from the National Party and so gaining 13 seats from the NP. The DP made a particularly strong comeback in Natal.

Voter support by party, 1987 and 1989 House of Assembly elections.

	1987			1989		
	Seats	Votes		Seats	Votes	
National Party	123	1,083,575	(53%)	93	1,053,523	(48%)
Conservative Party	22	549,916	(27%)	39	685,250	(31%)
Democratic Party	21*	343,017	(17%)	33	451,544	(21%)
Herstigte NP	-	62,888	(3%)	-	5,536	(2.5%)
Total	166	2,039,396		165**	2,195,853	

Source: *PFP Election Reviews* 1987/1989, Professor NJJ Olivier.

* The single NRP seat held in 1987, together with that of the single Independent, is included in this figure.

** One seat vacant in 1989.

Importantly, the DP not only recaptured most of the floating English vote but demonstrated that it held the potential to surpass the NP's support base. DP communications director James Selfe calculated that approximately 30% of the 1989 DP vote came from Afrikaners. In 1981 and 1987 the PFP had won approximately 4% of the Afrikaans vote. Thus the DP's increase of the Afrikaner vote, according to the *Weekly Mail*, 'was significant and indicated a clear shift'. The DP also won its first seat in a constituency with a majority of Afrikaners when Louis de Waal increased the liberal vote in North Rand by 4,789.

There were 21 constituencies where the DP vote improved on the results of the PFP or NRP in the 1987 election by a margin of more than 450 votes. And in reducing NP majorities in Durbanville, Westdene, Johannesburg West, Florida, Queenstown and Waterkloof, the DP showed clear indications of cutting into Afrikaans middle-class urban constituencies. The Democratic Party also demonstrated that its support base was not isolated to the Reef, the Cape Peninsula and Durban, but that it had also made inroads into the Eastern Cape.

My associates and I were surprised and pleased by the public and private responses to the election which we received on the Democratic Party's performance. Understandably, most were qualified: there was still a lot of work to be done in creating a fully fledged and inclusive constitutional system. But much had been achieved, and my associates and I knew what was still needed.

British Foreign Minister John Major wrote that we had given a formidable mandate for change. 'We look to the new government to take steps quickly towards everybody having the vote' (*Cape Times*, 8 September 1989). The response from the Bush administration in Washington was equally supportive of De Klerk's victory and of the election itself. An ANC statement on the elections concluded with: 'The people who voted, clearly voted for the process of dismantling apartheid' (*Sunday Star*, 10 September 1989). Several spokespersons responded for different Mass Democratic Movement organisations. Yunus Carrim said that 'Much will depend on the role of the Democratic Party. It will have to pin the NP down to creating a climate for the negotiations with the MDM. The DP has enormous potential to grow. However this will depend on the extent to which the DP is able to exert pressure to get genuine negotiations under way' (*Sunday Tribune*, 10 September 1989). Gael Neke, publicity secretary of the Five Freedoms Forum, stated: 'While there is no democracy, we can hope the Democratic Party will use its increased presence to reflect the concern and needs of the whole South African population within Parliament, while the MDM continues its pressure from without' (*Argus,* 8 September 1989). In his reaction, IDASA executive director Alex Boraine stated: 'The election result has changed the face of South African politics … and will ultimately force the government to steer the country in a new direction' (*Argus*, 8 September 1989).

All these statements to some degree or other affirmed the importance of parliamentary opposition as one of the strategies for the re-formation of the South African political system. And from the reactions of the extra-parliamentary actors it is clear that, in contrast to the 1987 debacle when the lone PFP failed dismally, the newly formed DP had demonstrated that a well-organised liberal parliamentary opposition party was one important element in a broad strategy for pressuring the government into instituting a meaningful programme for the normalisation of political activity.

My close associate and friend David Gant should have the last word. 'What can be inferred from the results of the election is that, while the DP

had demonstrated itself to be a significant player in the Parliamentary scene, it had also persuaded elements in the mass democratic movement (MDM) to take it seriously in terms of broad alliance-building. And in the final analysis, the Worrallite strategy was vindicated. The pivotal role played by Denis Worrall in 1987 in Helderberg and the formation of the Independent Party in 1988, inspired by his personal vision and courage, manifested itself in the 1989 elections and enabled the DP itself to become a significant player both inside and outside of Parliament in South Africa's rapidly changing political landscape.'

I had made it clear to the new DP constituency committee before the election that I wasn't going to change my family residence from Cape Town to Durban if elected but that I would have a presence in Durban. After all, my wife Anita's practice, which she had built up over the years, was in Cape Town and our boys were happily at school in Cape Town. And so it was that we bought a lovely 17th-floor apartment in the well-known Maluti complex with unimpeded views of the Indian Ocean, which Anita came to love. And for transport in Durban I bought one of the most fabulous cars made – an old Karmann Ghia – which I had professionally spray-painted light blue with a white top so that my constituents would know when I was in Durban, whether for the weekend or for a constituency meeting or presiding at a function.

I was sworn in as a member of Parliament on 13 September 1989 and Anita joined me in flying to Pretoria for F.W. de Klerk's inauguration on 20 September. President De Klerk opened Parliament on Friday, 2 February 1990. Parliament, of course, was not new to me. I had been the member for Cape Town Gardens and had been a Senator. But little did we know that this was going to be the start of a fascinating process which would see the end of Parliament as we had known it and the introduction of a wholly new, all-inclusive system of government.

PRESIDENT F.W. DE KLERK'S SPEECH AND THE RELEASE OF NELSON MANDELA

1990 would be a climactic year for South Africa, and for me personally it would be an important year in that I would find another and different way of expressing myself socially and politically.

What is clear is that the National Party got badly mauled in the September 1989 election, for the first time receiving less than 50% of the total white vote; and given the fundamental changes the situation called for from President De Klerk, he would be forced to look to the Democratic Party for support. This is exactly what he did by lumping together the NP and the DP vote, something no National Party leader had done before and so enabling him to claim over 70% in favour of reform. The result was that there was widespread speculation of big changes that would be made in the months leading up to the opening of Parliament on 2 February 1990. But only he and a few trusted Cabinet colleagues knew what to expect. In other words, he took the Cabinet into his confidence but not the party caucus. So there was as much wonderment, if not more, on National Party benches as there was generally among the broad public when De Klerk made his spectacular announcement releasing Nelson Mandela and other politicals from prison, lifting the ban on the ANC and the SACP and other organisations, announcing the abolition of certain critical apartheid legislation, and committing the

government to a negotiated political future.

From my parliamentary bench as the member for Durban Berea, I must confess to having shared every bit of the excitement and admiration for De Klerk's performance. The American journalist Patti Waldmeir in her excellent book *Anatomy of a Miracle* wrote of De Klerk's 'relentless pursuit of logic' which caused him to oppose P.W. Botha's piecemeal reforms. This is also how I knew him – clinically rational – and I will illustrate this with reference to two aspects – firstly, the unbanning of the Communist Party and, secondly, the manner and timing of the release of Nelson Mandela.

Given the National Party's long-standing anti-communism, this could not have been an easy decision. In fact, the unbanning of the Communist Party was the focal point of the right-wing Conservative Party's criticism of De Klerk's speech. But it was something that he understood had to be done because it clearly would otherwise have been an obstacle to the ANC joining full-fledged negotiations. And, as I can confirm as a participant in the constitutional negotiations, leading SACP members like Joe Slovo, Chris Hani and Ronnie Kasrils made profound contributions to our deliberations.

As regards the timing and manner of Nelson Mandela's release, this is something De Klerk gave a lot of thought to. Clearly, from a communications point of view, the timing of Mandela's release was of crucial importance. Had the government announced beforehand that the release would have taken place on 11 February, most of the international media would have jetted into South Africa on the 9th or the 10th and De Klerk's own speech would have been given only a small fraction of the coverage that it actually received. Instead, given the way the release was handled, it meant that for a whole week the government was able to keep the media ball in its court. It was able, with the support of the South African media and liberal organisations like the Democratic Party, to get across the fact that the country was in the process of a transformation or, as De Klerk put it, 'a paradigm shift'.

President De Klerk had two meetings with Mandela relevant to his release. The one was before his speech and the other after the speech. The government's preference was that he be released in Johannesburg, and to avoid the risk of an uncontrollable gathering, that the place and time of his release be kept a secret as long as possible. But, as De Klerk says, this was not acceptable to Mandela. He wanted to walk through the gates of the Victor Verster Prison as a free man. He also wanted his release to be delayed for at least a week so that he, his family and the ANC could make the necessary

preparations. And so the government was forced to compromise on the timing of his release. When after 27 years of incarceration Nelson Mandela, with a jubilant Winnie at his side, walked out of the Victor Verster Prison a free man, millions and millions of people all around the world were watching, many deeply moved, all applauding.

In a small way I reflected this in the first speech I made in the new Parliament on 8 February. I said President De Klerk's speech and its follow-up 'was a triumph for South Africa, not simply for the honourable State President. The international reaction, quite obviously, speaks very favourably for the measures that have been taken ... This speech is an acknowledgement that parliamentary politics and extra-parliamentary politics – struggle and system – are part of the same process. Secondly, it is an acknowledgement that the real issue facing us is not the reform of our society but its transformation. Thirdly, what flows from this speech is a recognition of the moral right of black South Africans to participate in the same political system as white South Africans. Fourthly, this speech signifies that for the first time our politics are no longer for some 9 million people (whites, coloureds and Asians) but are the politics of around 50 million people. Fifthly, the President's speech signified that we are out of the apartheid era and into a new era. And finally one asks the international community and international corporations to take note that whatever justification there may have been to punish South Africa and force it to change is past. Now the time has come to help South Africa build the post-apartheid South Africa.'

I have lost the exact date but it was about a fortnight after Nelson Mandela's release that I took a phone call at home, and I immediately recognised the voice. It was Nelson Mandela. After satisfying himself he was talking to me, he told me it was Madiba who was on the line, and the reason he was calling was that he wished to thank Anita and me for the Christmas card wishes which we had sent him in early December. He went on to say that he was sorry that he was talking to me over the telephone before we had received his card thanking us. After a chat of ten minutes or so, to which Anita was privy, I thanked him for the call and ended by asking him how I should address him in future. His response: 'You call me Madiba!'

Later in the month – in fact on Friday, 23 February – and with my two Democratic Party associates Zach de Beer and Wynand Malan, I was to meet with him in Johannesburg. Aside from giving interviews to both domestic and international media on an almost continuous basis, Mandela had been

seeing persons from all walks of life. From white schoolboys to members of the diplomatic corps, from leading business persons to representatives of virtually every political persuasion. And everybody who had met him had come away impressed. Part of the charm of these meetings is that they took place at the little house in Orlando West where he had lived before his incarceration. (He steered clear of the mansion which Winnie had built.) It was here that my parliamentary colleagues and I met with him that Friday. He was accompanied by Murphy Morobe, Cyril Ramaphosa and Valli Moosa, representing the UDF and the MDM. We gathered in the lounge, which barely accommodated the seven of us. We were there to discuss developments ahead; to explore areas of agreement and disagreement; and to try and establish a basis for future cooperation. I would have other meetings with him in very different situations, but as one who had no connections with him other than exchanges of Christmas greetings, I offer some personal impressions of him at that time.

What impressed me about Nelson Mandela was his modesty, his unpretentiousness, his lack of bitterness, and his very natural charm. It also struck me that he was a natural conservative. If his references to nationalisation reflected the ideological orthodoxy of the late 1950s and early 1960s, so did his emphasis on the importance of education, self-reliance and discipline.

Nelson Mandela also struck me as being a very formal man. When he explained that later that week he would be going off to various African capitals, before flying to Stockholm to see Oliver Tambo, who had been hospitalised as a result of a stroke, he referred to his old friend as 'Mr Tambo'. He also struck me as being a very cautious person. During the hour-long conversation he was reluctant to be drawn on policy matters or to offer any ideas about developments during the rest of the year. What was clear was that the ANC was not ready to get involved in full-scale negotiations. It needed time to consolidate its position and work out leadership positions. I got the impression that Nelson Mandela would not occupy a dominant role in a domestically re-established ANC. I suspected that his role would be that of elder statesman. The reason for this partly related to his age and personality; and partly to the political elites which had emerged in South Africa over the years – the trade unions, the Black Consciousness Movement, the UDF and other smaller but more radical organisations, and individuals (for example, Allan Boesak, Trevor Manuel and Mohammed Valli Moosa) who were looking to play a role in developing the new South Africa.

The months after De Klerk's speech and Mandela's release involved what I think is probably best described as a sorting out of issues and identification of how the parties would commence discussions. I had been appointed as the constitutional spokesperson for the DP, a role I shared with Colin Eglin, who was the party's main spokesperson on foreign affairs. While President De Klerk was kept busy implementing his commitment to repeal discriminatory laws, Nelson Mandela and his top aides were putting together their approach to the negotiations which were to come.

The formal negotiations were preceded by the Peace Process, and a National Peace Accord was signed by most political parties (and civil society organisations) on 14 September 1991. This laid the way for addressing not only the thousands of violent deaths that had been occurring, but also the foundations for the Convention for a Democratic South Africa (CODESA), which started in December 1991 at Kempton Park.

To give some idea of how complex the process was, by the time CODESA started little progress had been made in agreeing on what the mechanism there would be for drawing up a new constitution. The NP and the ANC found themselves deadlocked on this important matter. The ANC wanted an elected constituent assembly to do this, while the NP wanted an all-party conference to draft the document. Our own position as the DP, which was not involved in the discussions pre-CODESA, favoured a national convention, representing all sections of the population. But we would not have agreed that it be elected on a universal franchise basis but by proportional representation.

What also slowed things down was that both the National Party and the ANC quite correctly wanted to inform the international community of the commitments both organisations had made and their hopes for the future. So it was that first De Klerk and then Mandela made whistle-stop tours to key European capitals and Washington; and although this wasn't at the same level, it was agreed that I should get our point of view across. So it was that, accompanied by James Selfe, who was a great help in interpreting Democratic Party policy, I went to Paris, London (where I met with Margaret Thatcher), Lisbon and Rome. The essential message that we put across was conveyed in an international newsletter I wrote in December 1991: 'The world at large has warmed to the country. 1991 will be marked as the year the RSA broke out of its isolation. South Africa opened diplomatic or consular relations in the course of 1991 with 12 countries. Seven international airlines either

began flights into South Africa or are seeking to have scheduled flights to the country. Trade and commercial sanctions collapsed, and South African products reached markets undreamed of a few years ago.'

I might have added, with South African cricketers having just played in India, the basis was laid in 1991 for a dramatic return to international sport the next year: the Barcelona Games beckoned, rugby tours were on the cards, the International Grand Prix returned to Kyalami, and the Paris-to-Dakar rally would end in Cape Town in January 1992.

At the end of November 1991, at a meeting at the Holiday Inn near what was then Johannesburg International Airport an agreement was reached on the rules for the first multiparty conference, later called CODESA. It was agreed that decisions made would be reached through a vaguely defined concept of 'sufficient consensus', which was generally accepted to mean that at least the major parties – the National Party, the ANC and the IFP – would have to agree before a proposal could be adopted. However, CODESA's purpose was not to draw up a new constitution but to decide how that was to be done. This gives some idea of just how complicated the birth of the new South Africa actually was.

As the DP member of Parliament for Berea and a party spokesperson, I was a member of CODESA 1. CODESA 1 established five working groups to prepare the way for a secondary plenary conference – CODESA 2 – which started meeting in early 1992 but then came to a deadlock in June after the Boipatong massacre. Eventually the second round of negotiations was called the Multi-Party Negotiating Process (MPNP).

I didn't make much of a contribution as the real discussions took place between the ANC and the NP and then at top level. To me, the main advantage of participation in the negotiations was the individuals I met and got to know and with whom I would later have working relations outside politics. These were individuals like Joe Slovo, Pallo Jordan, Thabo Mbeki, Valli Moosa, Bantu Holomisa, Ronnie Kasrils, Cyril Ramaphosa, Chris Hani, Mosiuoa Lekota and others. I knew most of the government's delegates but was particularly impressed by the contribution of Gerrit Viljoen and Roelf Meyer. Viljoen was a brilliant Classics scholar whom I first met when we were both junior lecturers at Unisa. The strain of CODESA affected his health and led to his resignation and his death shortly afterwards. Roelf Meyer has an uncluttered mind and a tremendous capacity for developing personal relations. But I never really got to know him well and once deeply

offended him. There is a saying 'playing the man rather than the ball', which I think I generally managed to avoid. But there was an exception. I described Roelf in rather disparaging and undeserved terms in a House of Assembly debate. And if he reads this, he should take it as an overdue apology.

Quite understandably, given the critical issues involved and just what was at stake, the constitutional negotiations went haltingly, making enormous demands on all leaders but particularly on De Klerk and Mandela. This period was also characterised by intense internecine violence – which continued (albeit at a slower rate) even after the National Peace Accord had been signed. An added dimension was the increasingly bitter dispute over who was responsible for instigating the violence. These developments empowered the white right-wing to the point where De Klerk sensed serious problems, particularly from the results of a by-election in Potchefstroom, which had always been a safe National Party constituency and which the NP had won in the 1989 election with a majority of 2,000. This was reversed in the by-election when the Conservative Party won a majority of over 2,100 votes. In the face of what was a devastating result for the National Party and obviously for the negotiation process, De Klerk called a referendum of the white voters of South Africa for 17 March 1992. The simple question voters were invited to respond to was: 'Do you support the continuation of the reform process that the State President started on 2 February 1990 and which is aimed at a new constitution through negotiations?'

De Klerk writes in his memoirs that in the following weeks he campaigned vigorously for a yes vote throughout the country. So did my 34 DP parliamentary colleagues and I, and were it not for our commitment, total support and separate campaign De Klerk would not have gained the 69% of white voters who voted yes – something which De Klerk had the good sense to acknowledge.

The constitutional negotiation process, which I am sure many South Africans at the time will have found puzzling with its numerous stages, bodies and procedures, approved an Interim Constitution on 17 November 1993. This in turn was passed by the existing Parliament on 23 December and an election was set for 27 April 1994. With the passage of that legislation and the dissolution of Parliament, I effectively retired from parliamentary politics. In September I had told Zach de Beer, as leader of the DP, that I would not be coming back. He said he was sorry but didn't try to persuade me to change my mind. I was resigning not because of a lack of interest but

because, as Colin Eglin subsequently wrote when describing how different individuals were affected by the new constitution: 'Worrall, one of the former co-leaders, stayed on in Parliament but his political ardour waned as his interest turned towards a post-Parliamentary career in the private sector.' Early in January 1994 I therefore thanked the voters of Durban Berea but assured them of my continued support of the Democratic Party in the coming election.

On 17 December 1993, a matter of days before the dissolution of Parliament, I made my last parliamentary speech. Reading the Hansard report I am struck by the continuity of themes with the first speech I made in Parliament on 8 February 1990. I said the success of the constitution depended 'very largely on the kind of politics which the country will develop because, after all, politics fills the constitution. And given the nature of South Africa, and the kind of society we are, our history, our demography, our cultural make-up, the different political ideologies and our diverse experience, it is essential that we develop a politics of consensus in which both in substance and style, we stress areas of common agreement rather than seek points of difference. The process whereby this constitution, and the Transitional Executive Council which goes with it, have been created, has greatly helped establish a politics of this kind.'

Another theme I felt needed to be repeated related to the nature of South African society and what I saw as a compromise in our constitution-making. 'A fundamental compromise has been built into this constitution. It is the compromise between two broad approaches to the whole question of democracy in South Africa. Two academics have greatly figured in the discussion of democracy in South Africa over the past eight years. These are Arend Lijphart and Donald Horowitz. The two points of view have been very different. One said it was essential to recognize and use the different communities as building blocks for the future. The other has said that one must ignore all the different communities and hope that political mobilisation will bring them into the process and that, in this way, there will be a fair distribution of political power and political goods. The constitution represents a compromise between these points of view, because elements of consociational democracy have been built into it. There is a role for differently committed leaderships, and proportional representation figures strongly. There is a deliberate attempt at creating roles for all political parties and achieving the widest possible representation.' I went on to quote the American statesman

Thomas Jefferson, who said that politics has three principles – compromise, compromise and compromise. 'And if anybody knows the meaning of those words, it is those who participated in the negotiating process which brought about this constitution.'

There was, of course, never any possibility that the National Party would win the April 1994 election. This was something De Klerk acknowledged, and by Monday, 2 May, initial information from the Independent Electoral Commission and other sources had confirmed this. De Klerk, who had been monitoring the process from the NP's headquarters in Pretoria, decided to concede defeat. As one can imagine, this was an emotional moment. He congratulated Nelson Mandela and said that he was looking forward to working with him in the Government of National Unity. 'Despite our differences we have proved that we can work together … Mr Mandela has walked a long road and now stands at the top of the hill. A traveller would sit and admire the view. But the man of destiny knows that beyond that hill lies another and another. The journey is never complete. As you contemplate the next hill, I am holding out my hand to you in friendship and in cooperation.' This was one of the most moving speeches De Klerk had made. So we ended a chapter in our country's politics and a new one opened.

The full results of the first democratic elections were announced on Friday, 6 May. The ANC received 62.6%; the National Party received 20.6%; the IFP 10.5%; the Freedom Front 2.2%; and the Democratic Party 1.7%. The ANC thus had sufficient votes to ensure its presidential candidate would be elected.

Colin Eglin described the Democratic Party's performance as disappointing, and the general feeling within the party was that Zach de Beer should take responsibility for this. As Colin says, 'The dice were loaded against De Beer. He was up against De Klerk and Mandela, the most prominent leaders driving transformation and reconciliation. Millions had seen them debating on television – and rounding off by shaking hands as a symbol of mutual understanding and national unity. Zach, who remained a highly respected political leader, had not done particularly well. What people did not know was that he was under heavy medication for vascular and cardiac problems and contemplating retirement at an appropriate time after the election.'

It was left to David Gant, as chairman of the party, to advise Zach that the time had come for him to stand down. Next morning he handed in his resignation as an MP to the secretary of Parliament, and two weeks later, on

Saturday, 2 May, at a special DP meeting, Tony Leon was elected the new leader in preference to Ken Andrew, the only other candidate. I was naturally pleased that Tony found inspiration in the Helderberg election and what emerged from it. In his leadership acceptance speech he said: 'We may be a small party, but we can be the pivot of a realignment – at the radical centre of our politics. And if you doubt that we can do it, remember what Denis Worrall once achieved from a far smaller base than ours is today.'

CONCLUSION

Politics has been described 'as the art of the possible'. But I believe, no doubt idealistically, that all political activity should be undertaken as a means to a defined end or towards the achievement of a societal goal that embraces at the very least the notions of peace and prosperity for all, and value systems which include personal freedom, human dignity and the rule of law. And so the question arises at the end of my story: what, if anything, did my political activity achieve? And are there lessons to be learned from it? Put simply, did my political life and career make a difference?

I need to say that if indeed there are achievements, lessons, legacies and differences to be noted, it would be misleading to attribute these to me personally – because this book clearly shows how my political life has been hugely inspired, shaped and guided by my wife, my family, friends, colleagues, educators and countless others, some known to me, some not, who together are responsible for the outcome of my own political life and the positive changes in the South African political environment to which it may have contributed.

In the 1970s and 1980s political, social and economic change in South Africa became an urgent imperative. A continuation of the status quo could only have led to increasing unrest, economic regression, international isolation and deteriorating black–white relationships, even possible civil war. But the critical change needed was resisted by the government and most white South African citizens, who were inherently afraid of change, and who were unable to comprehend a viable alternative political system. That's how I saw it from the South African Embassy in London and what led to my resignation. That is how Dave Gant saw it from inside South Africa. And, of course, a good part of the book is about how we joined forces. As he puts it:

'The powerful and refreshing message with which, with Denis' lead, we went into the 1987 Helderberg election and the dramatic result achieved was the first indication that whites – English and Afrikaans-speaking – would embrace change and an all-inclusive democratic political dispensation.

'That election inspired the creation of the Independent Party with its rapidly growing support base, which was followed by endorsements by numerous high-profile individuals, black and white, throughout South Africa. And lest it be forgotten, it was the Helderberg election which sufficiently empowered the Independent Party to forge a merger with the fast-declining Progressive Federal Party and the peripheral but symbolically important extra-parliamentary movement of Wynand Malan. As is widely acknowledged, the resultant Democratic Party with Denis as one of its leaders was dramatically successful in the general election of 1989. A new political centre emerged which consequently played a significant role in the referendum which President De Klerk called and the reforms with which he proceeded, which led to the all-inclusive election of 1994 and the presidency of Nelson Mandela.'

So writes my friend Dave Gant. He might have added that the all-inclusive election of 1994 also saw the rebellious far-left, mainly black, and the ultra-conservative far-right, mainly white, reduced to insignificant and largely irrelevant political parties, with the centre holding strong and the Mandela and even Mbeki years showing promise over the long term. Meanwhile, the Democratic Party evolved under the leadership of Tony Leon, Helen Zille and Mmusi Maimane as the Democratic Alliance, a fully multiracial political organisation which is today the official opposition in South Africa.

To the extent that I, with my support base, contributed to this momentum and signalled the end of 'white only' politics, I have a sense of achievement and of making a difference. But sadly and ironically, the South Africa of today faces a new challenge which is as imperative and urgent as in the 1980s. The Zuma decade has left South Africans scarred by populism, racism, corruption and crime, and a completely debilitating joblessness with severely negative consequences especially for our youth. The challenge to Cyril Ramaphosa, whom I know to be a thoroughly capable, decent and modern man, is enormous – especially given his ethnic minority status and slim margin of support within antagonistic ruling party circles. And the fact that the country is less than a year away from a critical general election, with tough measures needed right now if the economy is to be turned around,

simply adds to the pressure that Ramaphosa and close associates like Pravin Gordhan, Nhlanhla Nene, Naledi Pandor and others are under.

Yet as in the 1980s, most South Africans recognise the need for change, reform, redress and redistribution. Perhaps what is required is the development of a consensus of the centre and a recognition that the current status quo is unsustainable, that the focus should be on the survival and well-being of the country at large, in effect a rallying call to do what is right rather than a pursuit of party or personal political power or self-enrichment. And here I believe the Leader of the Opposition, Mmusi Maimane, and the Democratic Alliance have a unique role to play. Proudly demonstrating good government as they have in the Western Cape and elsewhere where they gain majorities, they should acknowledge that at national level their chances of ruling directly are slight and they should throw their considerable intellectual weight behind Ramaphosa and his supporters. Aside from being the most productive strategy the DA can follow in the foreseeable future, it is a strategy that will accelerate the split in the ANC which some analysts believe is inevitable, and involve the DA in national government.

FURTHER READING

Readers in the United Kingdom and elsewhere may wish to know more of contemporary South African politics, and while there are dozens of worthwhile books I could recommend, here are two. A good background read is Max Du Preez's *A Rumour of Spring* and in my opinion an excellent look into the future is offered by Jakkie Cilliers in *Fate of the Nation: Three Scenarios for South Africa's Future*.

About the Author

Dr Denis Worrall (BA. Hons., MA (UCT) LLB (UNISA) PhD (Cornell)) is a business leader and academic in South Africa with extensive experience on multiple continents.

Since 1987, Dr Worrall has managed Omega Investment Research (Pty) Ltd and a UK-registered company of the same name. Dr Worrall is former Vice Chairman of the International Bank of Southern Africa (shareholders: Banque Bruxelles Lambert, Banque Nationale de Paris and Dresdner Bank); Managing Director of D.O.C. Finance S.A. (South Africa) (Pty) Ltd; former Chairman of Australian mining company Crown Diamonds N.L; a director of various private companies, and a consultant to the World Bank and several multi-national corporations.

In 2015 Dr Worrall initiated the founding of the on-line business service and newspaper, *Cape Messenger,* with the specific purpose of promoting the Western Cape.

A political scientist and lawyer by training, Dr Worrall has taught at universities in South Africa, Nigeria and the USA; edited the first general textbook on the South African Government and politics; practiced as an advocate; was in public life in South Africa from 1974 to 1994; and was South Africa's Ambassador to Australia (1982 – 1984) and the United Kingdom (1984 – 1987) when he resigned for political reasons. He was subsequently a founder and co-leader of the Democratic Party. He is married to Romanian-born Dr Anita Worrall, and the couple have three sons.

INDEX

C

Chris Heunis is congratulated by his supporters for his 39 margin out of more than 18 000 votes cast.

A matter of nuance . . . Fred Esterhuyse in the Vaderland.

Gary Player's support for me generated substantial publicity.

Mr. Harry Oppenheimer – a modern businessman with highly developed intellectual and cultural tastes and a great benefactor.

Denis Worrall from the balcony of his office overlooking Trafalgar Square.

WORRALL MET ... British Prime Minister Mrs Margaret Thatcher welcomes Democratic Party co-leader and former ambassador to London Dr Denis Worrall to 10 Downing Street before their talks yesterday.

Prime Minister Margaret Thatcher welcomes Democratic Party co-leader and former ambassador to London, Dr. Denis Worrall, to 10 Downing Street.

Worrall ... straight-talking in Stellenbosch